CREATING
LUCK

CREATING
LUCK

W

**Transform Your Living
Space and Your Life with
a Simple Formula**

E

S

Marcio Amaral

HAY HOUSE

Australia • Canada • Hong Kong • India
South Africa • United Kingdom • United States

First published and distributed in the United Kingdom by:
Hay House UK Ltd, 292B Kensal Rd, London W10 5BE.
Tel.: (44) 20 8962 1230; Fax: (44) 20 8962 1239. www.hayhouse.co.uk

Published and distributed in the United States of America by:
Hay House, Inc., PO Box 5100, Carlsbad, CA 92018-5100.
Tel.: (1) 760 431 7695 or (800) 654 5126; F
ax: (1) 760 431 6948 or (800) 650 5115. www.hayhouse.com

Published and distributed in Australia by:
Hay House Australia Ltd, 18/36 Ralph St, Alexandria NSW 2015.
Tel.: (61) 2 9669 4299; Fax: (61) 2 9669 4144. www.hayhouse.com.au

Published and distributed in the Republic of South Africa by:
Hay House SA (Pty), Ltd, PO Box 990, Witkoppen 2068.
Tel./Fax: (27) 11 467 8904. www.hayhouse.co.za

Published and distributed in India by:
Hay House Publishers India, Muskaan Complex, Plot No.3, B-2,
Vasant Kunj, New Delhi – 110 070. Tel.: (91) 11 4176 1620;
Fax: (91) 11 4176 1630. www.hayhouse.co.in

Distributed in Canada by:
Raincoast, 9050 Shaughnessy St, Vancouver, BC V6P 6E5.
Tel.: (1) 604 323 7100; Fax: (1) 604 323 2600

A catalogue record for this book is available from the British Library.

ISBN 978-1-84850-825-5

Printed and bound in Great Britain by CPI Group (UK) Ltd, Croydon, CR0 4YY

To the people I love the most, with thanks
for the support that has made me who I am
today: my father, Milton; my mum, Celia; my
big brother, Milton Filho; and above all the
man who taught me never to forget those who
have helped me, my uncle Glockner.

CONTENTS

Acknowledgements		*ix*
Introduction		*xi*
Chapter 1	Preparation	1
Chapter 2	The Three Energies	17
Part I	**Earth Energy**	
Chapter 3	What is Feng Shui?	37
Chapter 4	The Directions of Your Home	53
Chapter 5	Career	67
Chapter 6	Spirituality and Knowledge	75
Chapter 7	Family	81
Chapter 8	Wealth	87
Chapter 9	Inspiration, Reputation and Fame	97
Chapter 10	Love	103
Chapter 11	Creativity and Children	115
Chapter 12	Friends, Mentors and Networking	123
Chapter 13	Feng Shui Guidelines	129

Part II	**Human Energy**	
Chapter 14	Look Within	139
Part III	**Heaven Energy**	
Chapter 15	Connections	157
Chapter 16	Understanding Karma	171
Chapter 17	Creating Space for Change	183
Afterword	Finding Peace	191
Appendices:	I: Ming-gua Numbers	195
	II: The 12 Animals of the Chinese Horoscope	201
Resources		203

ACKNOWLEDGEMENTS

The idea behind writing this book is to bring out the happiness in people. I think we should always try to find the good in everyone and everything. Sometimes we will meet people who try to complicate life and we may get frustrated, but in my view life is simple and it is our desires that make it complicated. Still, life is eternal and I need no further proof of that. My training as a medium has been supported by Anthony Kesner and my fantastic classmates at the College of Psychic Studies in London. I also have to thank my teachers of feng shui: Roger Green, Great Grand Master Chan, Master Kajal Sheth and Jillian Stott. They all helped me to realize what first started as a dream.

I need to acknowledge the charisma and friendship of Darren Thomson and Lizzie Hutchins. I do believe that the best relationships and friendships are the ones where you have no secrets from each other and you can always be yourself. In those associations you have no right to judge, but you have the right to worry.

There is no use in connecting to people if you can't share, and that is why I have to say a huge thank-you to everyone who gave me support when writing this book.

INTRODUCTION

Is it possible to create luck? Can we generate good fortune and bring happiness, prosperity and love into our lives? Or is luck just something that some people have and others don't – something controlled by God, fate or another form of higher power? As someone who has studied feng shui for many years, I am utterly convinced that we can change and shape our luck, minimizing the bad and enhancing the good. My confidence stems from the fact that I have seen it time and again in the lives of my clients. Now I want to explain to you how we can all do it.

No matter how old you are, your life will never be the same once you learn how to create luck – if you are a young person, you will have an easier path through life, and if you are a more mature, discerning person like me, you will be able to appreciate your life much more. Remember, it is no coincidence that you are reading this book: the universe has brought it to you because you were asking for guidance.

Creating luck depends on energy, as energy generates the strength and vitality that shape your life. Studying feng shui for the past 18 years has taught me that everything is energy. This book will help you to understand and use it. You will learn how to feel it. It is there all around you, though you cannot see it, and just like the electricity and gas connections in your home, it makes your world bright and warm and makes things happen.

Energy follows intention, so creating luck is also about having a passion for living. What is your passion? What would you like to have more of in your life? How do you feel about your life right now? In this book you will learn about your feelings and how they correspond to the results you get.

As you start creating luck, 'coincidences' will start happening, but they will be your own power manifesting your desires. This book is a guide, but you will be the magician. You will learn that you have the power to create the life you want and nothing and no one can have power over you unless you let them.

So, it is vital that you prepare yourself for the changes you are about to make. The first chapter outlines how to do that, then I go on to explain how luck works, as it does have its own unique principles. Once you start applying these, as explained in the rest of the book, you will never go back to the way you were. You will be able to move forward – with optimism. Whereas optimism is easy, our challenges are as difficult as we make them.

Life is thought in action – what you practise, you will become. If you smile, you will become happier; if you help others, you will become more compassionate. Plant the right seeds and your life will blossom. Your hands may be empty to start with, but they are there to help you build the life you want, so don't be disheartened. All you need is the courage to step out and become a winner. This book will show you how.

CHAPTER 1

PREPARATION

So, are you ready to create luck, love and happiness? But wait – before you go ahead and create changes in your life, it's important to stop and reflect on where you are right now. That way, whatever changes you are hoping to make, you can lay down a firm foundation so they will be lasting.

Listen to Your Thoughts

Listening to our thoughts plays a large part in creating luck, because that way we come to know ourselves better, get in touch with our needs and wants, and gain answers to our questions. How well do you know yourself? Do you know what you really want in life? If not, how can you make it happen?

One way to get in touch with yourself is to start observing how you treat yourself. What do you eat and drink? What do you do to maintain your health? Are you on a self-destructive path, doing of things that will destroy your well-being, or are you taking care of yourself?

Listening to your thoughts can also teach you a lot about yourself and about your best way forward. It's interesting that many people stop listening during a conversation to analyze what is being said. Most misunderstandings arise this way. The same happens when we don't listen to ourselves. But if we remain engaged with our thoughts, our soul will be able to interact with us and supply the answers to our questions.

The best way to do this is to enjoy the thought process, so go somewhere nice, lie on the grass, look up at the sky and start thinking and dreaming. This is a very powerful way to get answers, but you must listen to what you get and pay attention to the feelings that come through, too. Afterwards, relax, write down anything that came to you so you don't forget and then wait and see what happens.

If you are worried, you definitely need to engage in some thought and let your soul bring you the solution. I remember worrying at one stage in my life about how to pay my rent and within just 30 minutes I had a thought about my bank account. I checked my statement and realized some of my bills were quarterly and wouldn't be paid that month, so I had the exact amount I needed to pay the rent after all. I had been worrying in vain. How lucky was that?!

Love Your Parents

Our parents play a very important part in our luck. The relationship we have with them counts for a great deal, because it generates our beliefs. Our parents have a lot of knowledge and wisdom too, and we benefit from learning from them, just as they benefit from learning from us, and through that energy our life can change just like magic.

What if we don't have a parent, or parents, or are adopted? Bear in mind that 'parents' doesn't mean just biological parents, but the people who stood by us as we were growing up.

When we are born, we are spiritual energy entering a physical body and this binds us to our parents. This means we may have chosen them before we arrived here or agreed to be with them for a particular reason. We all have the parents we were meant to have. If you think deeply, you will find a reason why you have the parents you have.

Whatever we have become is the result of the love between us and our parents. The nourishment that we had as a child will also be reflected in how we relate to people as friends and, especially, as partners. When we are in a relationship, we will treat our partner the way our parents treated us. We need to make sure we bring love into the equation so that we can nourish our partner and maintain those connections.

When I look back upon in my life, I can see how my relationship with my parents shaped the events that have brought me to where I am now. I was born in Brazil, of Italian descent, during the military revolution. It was hard for my family. My father used to have a café-restaurant, but he ended up closing it down. People didn't have the money to spend there.

Nevertheless, my father was always a charitable person and he changed a community with his attitude. He was always clearing out things that we didn't use and giving them away, and one day I asked him why. He told me, 'Your life is what you give to others, and giving demonstrates compassion.'

Just like that, a lesson was learned. My father has always said that we are living an eternal lesson and we should be kind to others but make sure they don't abuse us or treat us without respect. He has always stood up for himself and for what he believes is right. What an example to have!

When I was younger, I wanted to become a psychologist. When I told my parents, they told me to read the Bible. Fortunately, my auntie Celina, who was part of most of my childhood and adolescence, reassured me by saying that I was a natural psychologist.

I did read the Bible, however. It holds many secrets for the soul. I was searching for spiritual truths at that time, so much so that I went to India for six months and lived in Goa so that I could walk the path of Jesus, and after that I went to be a shepherd in Israel. That provided me with a lot of time to read and learn about myself and develop my outlook on life. All the travelling also made me culturally aware and I had the chance to learn about other religions. I realized that God was present in all of them.

After all the soul-searching, when I was 21 I chose to go back to a seed that my grandfather had placed in my heart when I was a child. One day he had taken me on a journey by plane from Rio to Sao Paulo and at that moment, I see now, the seeds were planted for my ambition to become a flight attendant.

I applied for many jobs, attended many interviews and knew I was the right candidate, but somehow I never got the job. This carried on for many months and all that time whenever I spoke to my mum she said she was afraid of me being on a plane that crashed.

One day when I called to tell her of yet more application failures, something occurred to me: my mother's beliefs were blocking my path. I needed to change the way she was thinking.

I told her that she should think that I was going to be happy as a flight attendant and that nothing was going to happen to me, and she should want me to get the job. Just like magic, two weeks later I was invited to join an airline as a member of the cabin crew.

This is a good example of how you need to work with your parents to activate your luck. It is important to let them know what you want to become, or do, or have in your life, and then get them wishing good things for you and repeating how successful they want you to be. Language has power, and if you communicate your deepest desires to your parents, these can become reality.

But what if you don't have a good relationship with your parents? What if you are afraid they *don't* want you to be successful? Don't let it hold you back! I know people who have had bad childhoods and difficult relationships with their parents and have still grown up to enjoy total success. Emotional hardship can transform us for the better, though it can also destroy us, especially if we carry it with us throughout our lives. To avoid this, we must focus on the good memories rather than the bad ones. So, if you didn't enjoy being with your parents when you were growing up, put those days behind you. You'll never be able to buy back those moments, but you'll always be able to let them go for free. Then, with the creation of a new present, the past will become just a thought – you will no longer be living there.

This subject is very delicate for many people, but it is important to deal with it, as it will clear the way to creating luck.

This process needs to start with forgiving yourself for any negative feelings you had towards your parents as a child. Children aren't responsible for what happens to them as they grow, but adults are responsible for dealing with the past and changing for the better.

As a child, you will love your parents, or try to, simply because they are your parents and part of you. If you feel you can't love them, it can have far-reaching effects. If you have difficulty loving others, for example, check how you feel about your parents. It does start with loving your parents first, no matter how they have behaved towards you.

If you feel like a victim and blame your parents for creating that, it's time to change it. Allow yourself to love them, even at a distance if necessary. We have all been hurt by our parents at some stage or other, but that hurt can be healed. If you resent your parents and blame them for the way your life has turned out, deal with it right now. Use a counsellor if you feel you need to, but do address this, as it is key to creating better luck in life.

If you feel your parents had little influence over you, analyze your relationship with them and see if you have become what they always said you would be. This is an interesting process in itself. So often what our parents think of us is what we become.

Ideally, our parents support us in our early years and are there to take all fear of life away. When they aren't there, it can be fatal, as fear can totally take over.

This leads us to one of the issues that we live with in our society today: bullying. No matter what age you are, it can happen to you. People who bully others obviously are very insecure and must be faced and dealt with so that the bullying will stop. Parental love plays an important role here, because the person doing the bullying has had to learn to defend themselves because their parents weren't there as a support for them. On the other hand, the person who is suffering the bullying, at whatever age, really needs their parents to help them to overcome the trauma.

Being provided with support by your parents is far more important than being provided with material things. My brother and I had a childhood with nothing, just our creative minds. For a long time my parents could just about pay for our books and clothes, but not afford anything extra. I was enjoying some quality time with my brother in London recently and he was reminiscing about one Christmas when we got one present between us. I was OK, as I was just four years old, but my brother, being three years older, understood the hardship.

Looking back now and discussing all of this, we realized that our parents didn't give us everything, but they did teach us the most important thing: how to love one another. We have always been a close family and we are always there for one another. We are so close that for the sake of love we accept one another's views even if we disagree.

My mother has always been very religious and traditional in her ways, and when my brother and I were growing up the most important thing for her was for us to have good manners. She brought us up well and I appreciate it, but as a child I asked her why I had to do things the way she wanted. Her answer was simple: I should always have people saying good things about me because that would resonate and the good things would come back to me. She was right, too – other people's opinions of us do affect our luck, as the energy around us becomes imprinted with positive and negative words. What she taught me was of real value.

In my time I have seen many unloved friends from privileged backgrounds ending up on drugs. If parents don't give love and attention to their children, what if a drug dealer does? As we all need love in our lives, that might just be the turning-point that leads to hardship, suffering or even death.

Life is complex and parents can let children down and vice versa. The love that flows between parents and children can be tinged with disappointment and frustration. But a parent must always leave the door open, no matter how badly their kids behave. If children think they are hated by their parents, this can lead to depression, and counselling has to arrive in time, otherwise suicide can be the result. Once a person, whether a child or an adult, has really made their mind up to commit suicide, you will never be able to spot them because they usually behave quite calmly and happily. That is because they have made their minds up and know they have an exit route. Most of the parents who suffer such a loss simply haven't seen it coming.

What is interesting is that when we are children we see our parents as our protectors and expect them to be perfect and fulfil our every need. Later, the joy in life is to realize that they were actually just humans trying their best.

As children, we are a reflection of our parents' emotional state, and as adults we demonstrate the quality of love that they showed to us. And they in turn would have been living as best they could with what was passed on to them by their own parents.

Parenthood is best learned by practising it, as my mum says. There are no good or bad parents, just parents who know how to nourish and parents who do not. They are both part of what cannot be changed, and that is the tie that binds parent and child.

So, if you feel you cannot love your parents, think of it this way: everyone deserves a second chance, including them. They will have done their best and given you the knowledge they had at that time. Their own upbringing may not have been filled with love. If you can, forgive them their mistakes.

Also remember that times and attitudes change, and so do people. You parents may be very different now from what you remember. It's worth giving them a chance.

Let the past go, forgive if need be and start sending your parents love from your heart. If you can't do it, get help, because this is the way to creating luck and it will change your whole life. If you can express your love to your parents, magic will happen immediately. Try it!

Don't worry if your parents have passed away, because their souls are just a step away and they will listen to you. They will help you, too. I see over and over people finding happiness after the loss of their parents and the reason for it is that their parents are doing for them what they couldn't do whilst here on Earth, and that includes becoming closer to them and loving them.

As we become adults and have our own lives, our connection with our parents can be weakened or even broken. That is when things may not go the way we want them to go. It is also the time when our parents need us most. So make the effort to strengthen the bond with your parents. Thank them for what they have done for you. That gratitude will bring you a direct connection to your soul ... and to luck.

If you have no connection with your parents, a nice way to start is by using your thoughts. What you can create by thought is limitless, and the reason for that is the spirit world makes the connections for you.

If you don't know how to demonstrate love for your parents, don't worry. Just start working out in your mind how you might do it. Inspiration will soon follow.

You will know one day that you had the perfect parents – perfect for the course that you chose to study in this university called life. And if you are able to love them, too, you will be well on the way to creating luck.

Teach Children How to Love

If you can, as well as showing love to your parents, spend time with child and teach them how to love. A child doesn't need a parent to show them how to love –

they can be taught by anyone who cares for them. It is about the energy of love, and unconditional love has no biological pattern to it.

Teaching others to love is an art. Teaching a child about generosity, goodness, kindness, sharing, respect and creativity is an act of love that we should focus on as the child grows. Who knows what the creativity will lead to? My brother used to build sandcastles and that is probably what turned him into one of the most respected civil engineers in São Paulo. I used to read a lot and was always a deep thinker, and here I am writing a book. When we teach a child to love they can become anything.

Recently I was talking to a good friend of mine who works as a teacher and has two children. I was surprised to hear this story about her younger son.

When he was seven years old he wasn't being very nice to another child. My friend saw him and immediately called him over for a chat. She told him that he had to be nice because there was an invisible energy watching over him and seeing everything he did, and if he did nice things for others he would get nice things coming back to him. Then she asked him to go and apologize to the other child and he did.

A few days later she was visiting a friend of hers, an elderly lady, and she took her son along with her. When they were leaving to go back home, the elderly friend gave him a box of sweets. He was delighted and my friend took the opportunity to say to him, 'You see, because you apologized to your friend, now the invisible world has sent you a present.'

Three years went by and her son was in the playground at school one day when my friend observed another child behaving badly towards him. In an instant her son said to the other boy, 'Be nice – there is an invisible force watching us and if we are nice we will get nice things.' Lesson learned!

It is never too late to change a child's life for the better, though younger children do recover from trauma more quickly. I was speaking recently to a social worker called Anna Lucia Massaro at Nosso Lar, the charity I support, and she explained to me that it is easier to work with children up to seven years old, as they forget experiences. Once they are over seven, emotions play a big part in their lives and traumatic experiences can be with them for ever.

We must not forget the wars going on in the world and the people suffering and dying. In war many children are left without parents and need extra care after so much misery and shock. Are these children going to grow up angry and vengeful? We need to care for them and then the exchange of energy will create peace and abundance. There are also so many children in the world in need of adoption and so many loving people out there who will make good parents, but bureaucracy can get in the way.

We need to take our passion for life and spread it as widely as possible. We are all here to love and be loved,

and learning to love ourselves and teaching others to
love is an art.

Prepare for Chaos

Finally: a warning. As you start to create luck, you need
to be prepared for chaos. The law of life is that to create
change we need to create a mess.

Let's say you are in your garden and you want to move a
plant. First you take it out of the ground, disturbing the
earth as you do so, then you disturb more earth as you
dig a fresh hole to put it in and after that you have to tidy
up both areas. Life is the same – when making changes,
we may find things are disrupted and even get worse to
begin with, but in time they will get better. All energies
need time to mature, no matter whether they are in our
house, in us or in our spiritual life.

When you are faced with disruption and stress, always seek
the advice of your friends for a different way of looking at
the situation. Take what is good for you and use it, but
remember, what is good for one person isn't good for all.
You need to be able to make up your own mind; never
place your friends on the spot to make a decision for you
or lay yourself open to control or power games.

Support from friends is an important part of creating
changes and your true friends will support you
unequivocally, even if they don't like your choices. If
a friend puts you down over your choices, consider

whether that friendship is worth maintaining. Toxic friends can cause your life to stagnate, as they don't want to move on themselves and they do want you to live their lives with them. There's no need to explain anything to anyone – just allow them to be themselves and move on from them. True friends will be there for you. They are like family – there to share both the joy and the pain. And the luck!

CHAPTER 2

THE THREE ENERGIES

You may have read many self-help books. I have, too. But over the years I realized that no book had ever taught all the principles of creating luck. That's why I decided to write one.

I really believe in these principles. I first discovered them when I started studying feng shui, the Chinese art of placement.

My first accreditation was with Roger Green, the first teacher to translate the feng shui formulas for the northern and southern hemispheres into English. He always stressed the importance of respect for nature. He now teaches feng shui and nutritional healing in New York (see Resources).

My second accreditation was with Great Grand Master Chan Kun Wah in the Chue style of feng shui. This convinced me of the importance of karma and once again emphasized respect for nature. In nature there is silence and it is from silence that you get your answers. Great Grand Master Chan taught me a lot of what I know about how to create luck. He comes from the hierarchy of Great Great Grand Master Chue and established the Chue Foundation, a body dedicated to feng shui research.

I took the accreditation in Chue-style feng shui with Master Kajal Sheth. Her gentle manner taught me a lot about getting results responsibly.

There are no books on the Chue style; you have to learn in Chinese and read the formulas on the Chinese compass to know how to use it, which limits the number of consultants around the world. The reason for this is to maintain the purity of the formulas.

The Chue style was actually prohibited back in imperial times and in order to get the information out from the emperors to the less fortunate, it was revealed secretly through sacred poems. Only those qualified could understand the poems, so very few were able to translate the information correctly. Great Great Grand Master Chue was one of those and he passed the information down to Great Grand Master Chan. Today the Chue style of feng shui has a reputation for delivering superb results.

Over the years I also learned the art of Chinese astrology. I was taught by Master Jillian Stott. She trained directly with Great Grand Master Chan and her work has proven very accurate. She is a tutor with angelic understanding who works directly with the Diana Cooper School of Angels.

When you combine astrology with feng shui, you get great results. I have now combined both with mediumship. More on this later – for now, just rest assured that by using the principles in this book you will be on the right path to creating luck.

Focus on Solutions

One fundamental principle is to focus on solutions, not on what is wrong. Energy follows intention, so concentrate on the solutions and see and feel the results you want as if they have already happened. Your solutions are also your intentions – the more you focus on what you want, the more the energy will follow.

In a business context, for example, the development of any new product must focus on satisfying the needs of the clients. So, if the staff have that aim in mind and then work out how to solve the challenges, the solutions will come. During my research I have used this approach with many companies and in some cases productivity has doubled. In a sense, the employees themselves are also the product, and if they are frustrated, it will reflect on the actual product. So the approach of the management towards the employees will either make or break the company.

If you focus on solutions, you will save 50 per cent of your energy. You will no longer be feeding the challenge, so it will no longer be draining you and you will have the willpower and the strength to make changes more quickly.

Always remember that *energy follows intention*, so focus on getting great results.

The Key to Creating Luck

So, now you are focusing on solutions, here is the key to creating luck. It is very simple: you must balance your Earth, Human and Heaven energies.

What does this mean? Energy, as I explained earlier, is what gives you strength and vitality. It is composed of three different forms:

- The first is *Earth energy*.

- The second is what connects Earth and Heaven: *Human energy*.

- The third and most important is *Heaven energy*.

Each form of energy makes up 33 per cent of all the energy available to us and there is a rogue element of 1 per cent.

We will take a look at the different energies to see how they work and how we can make them work well together.

Earth Energy

Wherever you are at present, think about the world. Think about the two hemispheres, opposite each other, two halves of one whole. How perfect is that?

Now think about your home. Is it nice? Is there a garden? When you are inside your home, how do you feel? Can you see Heaven from the window?

Earth energy shapes our environment: the Earth itself. It also influences our home in many ways: how we look after it, how clean it is, how tidy, the location, the view from the windows. We may find that we are having eye problems, for example, and in our home the windows are dirty.

If you aren't happy with your home, there is an imbalance for a start. If you wish to move to another home, though, I must make it clear that you must first create balance in the home you have. There are many ways to do it. Think about how you can learn to love it.

The home is very important, as it holds a lot of our energy. It usually reflects our subconscious and in my experience the artwork can be particularly significant.

A long time ago I was called to a home in London to help a very friendly couple, both extremely intelligent, with no kids. They got on very well normally, but when it came to matters of the bedroom they were always arguing. They did love each other, but it had got to the point where they were thinking of divorce.

I checked their home and it was very stylish, with very expensive artwork all around. I went to the direction related to relationships downstairs and found a living room where they spent time together. I then went upstairs and in the relationship direction, quite amusingly on the wall opposite their marital bed, they had a picture of a really rough sea with a ship sinking.

That picture was swiftly replaced by an image of a romantic couple and within three months I heard my clients were getting along much better and no longer considering divorce. It is amazing how people can reproduce their artwork in their own lives.

What we have in our home can have a strong impact on our lives in many ways. I had a client once who wanted a relationship, but none of the guys she met ever stayed in her life for long. When I assessed her home, I discovered it had no space for a man. Her bedroom was nice, but very girly, with no male energy at all. There was just one bedside table. The artwork consisted of pictures of women. There were a lot of single objects as ornaments. You get the idea...

I explained to her that we would work on the male direction of both the interior and exterior of the home. We went to the garden and placed a statue of a Roman god there and inside the home we put up a picture of her favourite rock star. We put another bedside table in the bedroom and introduced a pair of bedside lights, one on each table. We also selected the perfect dates to make these changes.

These were just basic changes, but subconsciously they started activating my client's luck. Just as she was losing hope of ever meeting a suitable man, a friend from work introduced her to a soldier who happened to like the same rock star as she did, so they decided to go to a show together, and after the show – well, the rest, as they say, is history. They are now married with one child.

The influence that buildings have over us is quite interesting, too. I recently completed research on an apartment building where the male energy was missing from the design on the inside. The only couple in the building lived on the ground floor and they were lesbians. All the other apartments were inhabited by single women.

Energy is all around us and it is time for us to start feeling it and leave behind the belief that what we see is all that exists.

Earth energy affects the quality of our life in many ways, apart from the home. We take the food we eat from the Earth, and if we poison that, it will affect the quality of our physical life. On the other hand, drinking water and taking in the minerals that come from the Earth will help our health, and that, too, is all part of creating luck. Remember that the laws of nature rule the Earth, and that means they have power over us, too. So respect them!

Human Energy

Human energy is all about us as human beings and our interaction with the world. It is about how we listen to ourselves and make our own decisions.

For most of us, however, this energy lies dormant because we are born into tribes and our upbringing results in us controlling our Human energy and going along with the tribe. By 'tribe' I mean our culture, friends, family, religion and education. These all mould our beliefs. We belong to many different tribes during our lives.

It is all too easy to take on board the beliefs of our tribe and not get in touch with our own Human energy. It is perfectly normal to want to fit in. It is accommodating and safe, and we can get very insecure when we have to go out on our own, but if we want to create luck we do have to follow our own individual path. Inside all of us there is a powerful spirit waiting to come out.

One of the points of this book is to show you that you can step out of your tribe, be yourself and do whatever you feel is right for you. It is fine to belong to a tribe, but you shouldn't let it manage your life. Many people lose their real purpose when they start following others' practices and customs. You should manage your own life at all times. You can make use of religious or other faith to deal with fear, but the most important thing is to seek the answers inside yourself and trust the feelings that will come from your soul. Human energy is all about trusting yourself.

Human energy is also expressed in how you look after yourself – or not. If you are going through addiction in any way at present, especially addiction to cigarettes or alcohol, remember that the substance you are addicted to is more powerful than you are and is making you a prisoner. Who wants that?!

My father smoked from the age of 15 to 53. I often asked him to stop, but he used to say that if you enjoyed it, it didn't harm you. Then one day he woke up and found he wasn't enjoying it anymore. His willpower took over and was stronger than the cigarettes, so it was easy for him to stop smoking. He is now 75 and very healthy. Willpower is often underestimated, yet it can be a vital factor not only in breaking free of addiction but also in creating luck.

Another way of attracting luck is choosing to be nice, both to ourselves and to others. Sometimes we are affected by outside influences and can find it difficult to remain calm and good-natured, but if we aim for peace and harmony in all situations, peace and harmony will be reflected back to us.

This isn't to say we shouldn't be assertive when necessary. Assertiveness is a great quality to have, as it can clarify issues and assertive people always gain respect. In a working situation it can often be appropriate.

Don't let it go too far, however. Life isn't a competition and your luck and success will depend on how in tune you are with yourself, not on what other people are doing. When you waste time worrying about other people, you lose precious energy that can be used to improve your own life.

So much of Human energy is about making connections – within ourselves, between ourselves and others, and between Heaven and Earth. When we have low self-esteem, however, we aren't able to connect properly with other people, so we aren't good at negotiating our way through either our emotional or business life. That insecurity is then imprinted in our aura and we set ourselves up for failure. Our home will also reflect the way we feel and is likely to become dirty and messy. Living in such an environment will eventually cause our personal life to stagnate. Organized mess is good for creativity, but dirty mess is not.

If you find yourself in this situation, start by treating yourself kindly. That way you will be able to build the confidence to make more changes.

Talking of confidence, I would like at this point to mention vanity. It is good to look your best and feel confident, but don't make your appearance the focus of your life, as it can become a true addiction, especially when you get older. If you feel addicted to the way you look, get some therapy, because you need to accept yourself so that your soul is able to reside in your body peacefully. No matter what is bothering you, you need to establish communication with your soul, and that is more important than what you look like. Happiness lies within, not in external appearances.

All of us need to stop searching for happiness in what we don't have and be grateful for what we do have. If we focus on being healthy, giving and receiving love and above all gaining peace of mind, we will be sure to activate luck.

Here is an exercise to get in touch with your Human energy:

Look at yourself in the mirror. It is important that you get in touch with your image and are happy with what you see.

Still looking in the mirror, go back and revisit some of your past experiences in your head. Look at the way you behaved. See yourself as if you were on TV. Stand firm, look yourself in the eyes and feel your spirit. Go beyond your physical looks and try to see your body as a vessel.

Whatever you feel in this experience is your reflection to the world, your way of expressing the Human qualities within you.

And beyond those Human qualities, we all have a soul inside ourselves and that soul is perfect – which leads on to the third form of energy.

Heaven Energy

This is the most important energy, as it makes everything happen! It activates Earth and Human energy and is the secret to success. The key is to connect to it and to bring it into balance with our Earth and Human energies.

Heaven energy is all about our spirituality, which may be expressed in many ways, either through traditional religion or in a more idiosyncratic manner. I have always believed that whatever religion you have been raised in will have power over your life. You will never stop being that religion. Whether you choose to follow it is up to you, but it can be used if you want to activate your Heaven energy.

You don't need to be religious to be spiritual, however. I know many people who go to church regularly but aren't particularly nice people. Actually they go to church for the socializing. A truly religious person is also spiritual, but it isn't necessary to have a religion – the main thing is to understand that there is a soul inside us. When we realize that, we are empowered.

The key is to connect to Heaven energy and express it in our life – or, rather, to *know* that we are connected to Heaven energy, as we are all spirits and already do connect, but maybe without knowing it. Whenever we think, we are making a spiritual connection – we are actually talking to Heaven. If you find that hard to accept, start observing how many answers you get 'out of nowhere', especially when you are worried. You will know you have been answered when you have a feeling, a hunch, a gut instinct about what to do. If you follow that hunch, the results will make sense eventually, even if there is a creative mess to be made in the meantime.

Intuition plays a big part in connecting with Heaven energy. We feel it in the stomach area; it is a meeting-point of spirit and body. As well as putting us in touch with our spirit, it will improve the choices we make in life. In fact there are no wrong choices, as all experiences are there for a purpose, but some are easier than others.

We all behave in different ways when we are getting in touch with our spirit because each of us is unique. When I help people with feng shui, I call my Chinese astrology Master Jillian Stott to draw up a horoscope for them. That alone proves to me that every single one of us is different and that our destiny is influenced by where and when we were born.

Heaven energy and the movement of the stars do play a part in our lives. The proof of that is in the cycles of the moon. People get very sensitive at full moon, at new moon they plan changes like crazy and when the waning of the moon arrives, they can become more pessimistic and get upset about things.

Something I often find is that people lose touch with their spirit through a bad experience. The hurt and sadness will often result in them choosing to live their lives according to an archetype. Usually you know you are living an archetypal life when you are mirroring or comparing your life to that of someone very significant in your tribal beliefs. Let's take Jesus as an example. He sacrificed his life for others, so in this case you would be sacrificing yourself for others without expecting anything in return.

When something like this happens, the universe can stop you short to give you a chance to heal and reconnect. I have a good friend who is a super mother, the most amazing woman. She has four kids, all very polite and studious, and she supports them all the way. At one point, however, she was just too busy – driving the kids to school, to sports events, to extra classes, and so on, without taking a proper rest. It was all too much and she was drained of energy.

The family went on holiday and when they arrived at their holiday home my friend went to close the gates so the children wouldn't venture out of the garden. The gates were loose, due to refurbishment, and they fell on top of her, injuring her shoulders and leaving her confined to bed and her husband having to get in extra help.

Later on, when we met one morning, she confided that she had been living life with very little sleep, but it was only after the accident that she realized her attitude was jeopardizing the people around her. The accident was the way the universe stopped her.

Don't wait for the universe to stop you. If you feel you aren't living your own life, or you have had an experience that might have taken your spirit away from your body – especially one involving hurt and resentment – you must make sure that you start meditating to bring yourself back to the present. It can be something as simple as saying your name in your head and asking yourself to be present.

This can also be a process of forgiveness, for when we resent people who have hurt us or experiences that have happened to us, the only person we are harming is ourselves.

On one occasion my father went through a bad time when a work associate took his job from him. I felt bad for him because he had worked so hard and had lost everything. The universe arranged for us to meet on a bus journey from São Paulo to the countryside. We happened to go for the same bus by chance and ended up sitting together for two hours. That journey was to teach me the biggest lesson that I could ever have in life.

I told my father that I wasn't happy about what had happened to him.

He told me, 'Don't worry – my associate has a very unhappy life. Maybe my job will help to make it better. He needs it more than I do.'

I see now that my father had totally forgiven his associate and put the experience behind him. He hadn't let the stress ruin his peace of mind and he trusted that he wasn't going to go without.

In fact, after that loss, my father moved on to better things very quickly. I now understand that because he hadn't held on to the experience the universe brought a better one for him. And he became very successful in his new business.

If you resent something that has happened to you and cannot forgive, it means that you lack love, support and understanding. Try to develop them in yourself and you will find that forgiveness will become easier. If the past becomes too difficult to deal with, use spiritual healing or Reiki, and remember that there is power in surrendering. The way to surrender is to accept yourself, including all the good and bad that has happened to you, and then act to make your life better.

When you truly bring love into your life, forgiveness won't be difficult because you will have the answer as to why things have happened to you and the lessons you were meant to learn.

Creating luck is about living in the present, so learn to forgive and move forward – but don't go too fast into the future, make the most of today. There is an old saying: 'Life is short but the art is long.'

Above all, fear not: let your soul out of its cage!

Yin and Yang

The three energies – Earth, Human and Heaven – are divided into two qualities which are called yin and yang, and they help the balancing of the energies.

Yin is classified as feminine. It is quiet and calming, cold and gentle. It relates to darker colours and stillness. A mountain, for example, doesn't move and can be classified as a yin feature of the landscape. Yin can act to produce peace, passivity and stillness when you are balancing energies.

Yang is classified as masculine. It is lively and active. It relates to bright colours and movement. It is hot and active. Yang can act to produce action, assertiveness and movement when you are balancing energies.

How the balancing works is that if one side of something is yin, the other has to be yang. This works very well in our home (Earth energy), in our body (Human energy) and also as a spiritual guide (Heaven energy).

In other areas, the yin and yang qualities are balanced in other ways. As an example, a hospital building has yin energy and the nurses and doctors are the yang energy that balances this. When we are sick, we need peace and quiet, and a hospital provides that, but we also need the assertive energy of the nurses and doctors to make us better.

To take another example, if we go to church we will experience the yin energy of the building and we will be the living yang energy, which is why we will feel good when we are inside the church.

Whether we are using Earth, Human or Heaven energy, it is important to observe that the yin and yang are always balanced.

If we are working with Earth energy, it is very important to observe the flow of energy, especially if a house is very cluttered. We must always make room to move around a house, making sure we don't have obstacles on our path and can move freely. That way our life path will be easier.

If we are balancing our Human energy through the yin and yang of our body, any imbalance will usually be manifested through pain. The best professionals to help will be acupuncturists. They can release the yang energy that moves around our yin body.

If we are balancing our Heaven energy, what will usually be happening is that we are too yang and life is turbulent, active and stressful, so to create balance we will need peace and quiet, meditation or prayer. This will help our communication with the soul and so balance our yin energy.

Creating luck is about balancing all three forms of energy, Earth, Human and Heaven. There is no point in having a perfect home and being healthy if we aren't in tune with our spirituality. To be totally successful, we must connect with the area that we tend to neglect. Earth and Human energies can usually be mastered, but Heaven energy is often harder, because people associate it with religion and dismiss it from their lives. But quite simply Heaven energy is about connecting to the soul inside us and that soul connecting to the infinity of the universe. Then all the energy can flow and we will find luck coming into our life.

To begin with, however, let's look at Earth energy and how we can balance our home environment through the ancient art of feng shui.

N

NW

NE

PART I
EARTH ENERGY

W

E

SW

SE

S

'Life is short, but the art is long.'
ANONYMOUS

CHAPTER 3

WHAT IS FENG SHUI?

When tackling a subject as complex and richly textured as feng shui, it's always hard to know where to start. So, let's start at the beginning.

Feng shui is the Chinese name given to the art of placement. It emerged from the imperial palaces of ancient China, where the feng shui master was seen as a kind of magician, possessing a deep and powerful knowledge that had been passed down from master to student for thousands of years.

What is the 'art of placement'? Fundamentally, I see it as an art that creates luck. A skilled feng shui consultant will apply it to homes, schools, hospitals or businesses to help generate good luck. This luck, in turn, will lead to all the wonderful things people seek when they turn to feng shui – love, happiness, inner peace, health and prosperity.

In feng shui, we believe we must attend to each of the three energies to transform our lives. For example, to create Earth luck, you can ask a feng shui consultant to find the perfect property for you and to help you create the perfect outer and inner space to maximize your Earth luck. But the other energies – Human and Heaven – and the interaction between all three are equally important. If you focus solely on Earth energy, your luck will be temporary. So you might earn plenty of money, but it will slip away. And of course Human energy is essential, because if you don't attend to your physical and psychological health, what good is money? Who wants to be rich but sick, or wealthy but miserable? Ultimately, illness, bad fortune, lack of love and other issues are connected to Heaven energy, because if you are fighting against fate or leading a life that isn't right for you, your energy will drain away. For example, someone who's doing a job they hate just to put food on the table for their kids or is stuck in a marriage that is making them unhappy will feel trapped – as if their spirit is locked in a cage. Eventually, after a few years, it will catch up with them. They will lose all of their spiritual power and be left with the body, which is after all just meat and bones. Illness will inevitably follow.

This book aims to give you the feng shui basics that will provide you with immediate changes, but in time, as things improve, I do advise using the Chu Foundation website (see Resources) to obtain a full evaluation with an accredited consultant.

A few simple changes can have a dramatic effect, however. For example, I remember visiting the two-storey house of

Beth, a woman in her early thirties. She wanted to move on in her life, especially to find a new job, because she felt undervalued and as though she was always fighting her boss. To address her future and her wealth, I needed to tackle the front of her property, so I immediately checked that area and found that she had two enormous rubbish bins next to her front door. She also had a huge spiky plant covering the front window.

I first moved the bins to the back of the house, to a special area she had made for them. This immediately took away her negative feelings about the future. I also wanted her to move or cut back the spiky plant, but she wasn't keen, because she felt it protected the front window from burglars.

Two weeks later she called me. She said she was feeling amazing and was brimming with ideas for the future. The only problem was that she was still bickering with her boss. Had she moved the spiky plant? What do you think?

This highlights a common problem with feng shui – after my consultations, clients often call me and say it didn't work. I then ask them whether they have done what I recommended, and guess what they say? 'No, Marcio, not yet.'

I think this is indicative of the fact that many people are afraid of success, so hang on desperately to what feels safe to them. Our properties make us feel secure, but they may, in fact, be limiting us. That's why, when nothing else is working, we need to be bold and step out into the unknown.

So I asked Beth if she was finally willing to move the spiky plant from the front entrance to the back of the house. She agreed – and here's the amazing bit – the future opened its door to her and she got the job of her dreams. What's more, she didn't even have to look for it: she was head-hunted.

One final point: when we moved the plant, we chose the perfect date so we would be in coordination with the universe and her luck would change.

Initial Impressions

In the Chue school of feng shui, there is no one-size-fits-all approach. Each consultation is designed uniquely for the owner of a particular property, depending on that person's astrology.

Chinese Astrology

We use Chinese astrology to combine our Heaven luck with our Earth and Human luck. The method we use is called the Four Pillars of Destiny and it is based on the date and time of birth. This method can predict good and bad times, and therefore help a person to manipulate their luck by using a specific integration of energy at a specific time. Usually a master will draw up someone's chart to help them with what they are seeking to do, whether that be finding a partner, getting married, having a child, starting a business or selling a business.

There are some similarities with western astrology, but this is a completely different method of using astrology. It can be more accurate on prediction and timing. It is based on the elements coming into our lives at specific times – earth, metal, water, wood or fire.

As an example, I had a client who was born in an earth year. She was having a really difficult time finding a partner and when we got her horoscope done we discovered that she would only establish a firm relationship when wood energy entered her life. When we looked at the horoscope, we saw that wood energy would come in two years after the consultation and at that time marriage would come to her.

I helped her with her home's feng shui and we worked hard in the southwest, which was the relationships area for her as she lived in the northern hemisphere. That area was a spare room full of clothes. We decluttered it and painted it in pastel colours, then put up a fantastic picture of Andy Garcia, as she was a fan of his.

Now she knew her horoscope, she decided to stop searching for a partner there and then and relaxed, and by chance four months later she was invited to a dinner party that led to her meeting a work colleague. He was from Cyprus, had black hair and had very similar features to Andy Garcia. In due course the wood element entered her life and during those five years they got married. She was 47 years old and wanted a child. Fortunately, during that same period this was also possible through fertility treatment. That five-year period was very lucky for her love and family life and with the aid of Chinese astrology she was able to ensure her timing was perfect.

Once we have checked out a person's astrology, we then focus on the aspects of their life that they feel need addressing. I find that the most common aspect is money, especially in tough economic times like these. In simple terms, we believe that the front of a property embodies money, while the back embodies health. So if I were finding a property for someone, that's the first thing I would consider – how does that property sit? What is its shape? There are several basic areas to look at.

The Hemispheres

Please note that in feng shui we take into consideration the hemispheres of the world. The northern hemisphere has its reflection on the southern side, just like a mirror.

In the northern hemisphere the sun rises in the east, moves to the south and sets in the west. In the southern hemisphere the sun rises in the east, moves to the north and sets in the west. This difference means that the yin and yang energies are opposite and this affects our classification of the directions of the house. As an example, in the northern hemisphere the career energy is in the north and in the southern hemisphere it is in the south.

The Directions

One of the most important things to consider is the direction in which the property faces, as well as the trees and other vegetation that surround it, its relationship with the surrounding streets, and so on.

It is important to observe that 70 per cent of the effect a particular property has on us comes from outside the property – it is the result of what we look out at and what is coming towards us. The other 30 per cent stems from the inside of the property. That has a direct effect on our subconscious.

It's important to stress that there is no 'right' or 'wrong' direction for a property to face – luck is dependent on our own personal reaction to the directions. Further along you will use the Eight Mansions system to discover your personal lucky and unlucky directions. If your property faces one of your personal unlucky directions, that may be the cause of your challenges. The Chue school of feng shui does have a very personal approach.

Energy Flow

There are two types of energy flow, the *chi* and the *sha*. The *chi* energizes everything in a positive way. The *sha* is the opposite; it is to do with the manifestation of issues and challenges. We classify it as bad *chi*.

Inside our body, the *chi* also relates to our blood vessels and the way energy flows through us. Outside our homes and workplaces, it relates to the environment. Observe the shapes that surround your property. Is there a river or a road that is shaped like a river? Does the energy flow freely? How does it come to your door? Is there a path?

Are there rows of plants lining its way? If you live in an apartment, what do you see outside? Pleasant views will bring the *chi*; ugly views will bring the *sha*.

I remember visiting a client who had a house facing a very dilapidated building. That building was located in the north in the northern hemisphere, the direction that is related to the mother, i.e. the woman in the home. This woman was suffering with depression, couldn't see a way forward and felt as if she was broken in pieces inside in a way she couldn't explain.

Eventually the dilapidated building was taken down and I happened to talk to the client a while later. She told me that once the building was no longer there she felt her future was clear and she had come together in some way. She was now teaching yoga and feeling totally renewed.

When we are creating luck we need to check the energy flow around us. Remember, every challenge has a solution and we must focus on that solution.

The Elements

In feng shui we follow the Chinese system of five elements. These are:

- water
- wood
- fire

- earth

- metal

The elements interact with each other both constructively and destructively and if there is a clash of elements, that could be the cause of our challenges.

I remember visiting a house in north London where the wife had been very sick. I arrived at the property and immediately started analyzing it by opening all the windows and looking outside for anything that could be affecting the energy.

It was an apartment, and when I opened a window in the north I noticed that opposite there was an electrical company with several masts. As I mentioned earlier, the north outside a property in the northern hemisphere relates to the woman in the property; in that direction water rules. Here the fire element was prominent, so it clashed with the water, making the woman of the house sick.

The History of the Home

Always try and find out the history of your property. What happened to it before you moved in? Was it a hospital? Funeral parlour? Police station? Who were the previous occupants?

As well as our own energy, a home tends to keep the energy of the people who lived there before. For example, I have had clients who have moved into a house where the previous owners divorced and then they have divorced as well. It is important to balance the energy so that we don't suffer the same misfortunes as those who lived in our properties before us.

That is when a good cleansing can be helpful. So let's move on to decluttering and spring cleaning.

First Steps

Decluttering

When you start analyzing a property, it's amazing what you find. Some houses have rubbish stacked up outside, others have spiky plants covering the windows or a tree that's blocking all the light and energy from entering the home. Also, because the rear of a home embodies health, that's the most important area – but that's where most people put all their junk and clutter, the mess that represents their past, both physical and symbolic. Often one of my first tasks is getting people to clear out that junk and so let go of mistakes and disappointments that are holding them back, keeping them trapped in the past, unable to move on.

That leads us into one of the simplest but most powerful feng shui techniques anyone can employ: decluttering and letting go. First comes the intention to change, the desire to transform an unfulfilling aspect of your life. Once you commit to making that change, the next step is to let go of all the stuff you think you can't live without but in reality is blocking your path. I always think that anything you haven't used for six months, you can't really need, so that's a good place to start. Open up all those dusty boxes in your loft or basement and give what you can to charity or have a car-boot sale.

Look around your house and apply the same principle to clothes you never wear, books you never read and knick-knacks you don't actually like but have never bothered to throw out. Trust me, you won't miss any of these unloved possessions and you will create so much space, light and positive energy in your home.

Don't donate things you don't like to charity shops, though. If something wasn't good for you, it isn't going to be good for others. Only donate items you truly believe will make someone happy. This way the charity shop will sell more.

We tend to buy ornaments that accumulate dust, especially when we are on holiday, as we want a memento to remind us of where we have been. What is really funny, though, is that it is actually best to give these things to other people. They will love being remembered on your holiday and believe me you will get a few objects back, so you don't need to buy any for yourself at all. I find pictures on Facebook and Twitter much better for keeping memories, as they take no space and accumulate no dust.

Another thing I advise is donating to charity any foreign currency you aren't likely to be able to use for a long time. Most airlines make a collection now and that can be of major help to many different causes.

Spring Cleaning the Home

Once you have decluttered, if you want to add some love, light and space to your home, spring cleaning will give you some amazing results.

Think of the home as a person with a soul: the windows are the eyes of the soul, the main door is the mouth, the structure is the spine and each room an organ of the body. Focus on making this body and soul healthy and clean.

Don't just focus, in fact: talk to your home as well. Your home provides you with protection and will also dictate the flow of your intuition. You will have many ideas in your home, so love it and make it sparkling clean. The results will be immediate and as the energy starts flowing, you will feel amazing. The reason for this is that when we don't activate a room, the energy stagnates. So, make everything clean and fresh and open the windows and bring in air and light so things start moving again.

It's interesting that an untended part of a home usually corresponds to an untended part of a life. So, if you want your whole life to move forward, get cleaning!

After that, if necessary, paint the walls. Once that is complete, cleanse the space by burning a form of incense in each room, making wishes as you light it.

You could also use sage sticks to clear the space; they tend to be effective. When you light them and pass the smoke around the environment it clears any stagnant energy and takes it to Heaven. As the smoke leaves, it takes all the past of the house with it. This practice will bring a soul to the property and in turn the property will help you to prosper.

You could also ask a priest to bless your home or use a space-clearing consultant or a geopathic stress consultant to check out the Earth energies around your property and their effects upon it (see Resources).

Spring Cleaning the Mind

When you have cleaned your home, you need to start cleaning your mind, so I recommend the following exercise. Be honest with yourself throughout – and enjoy it.

- Wait for the last three days of the waning of the moon, because that's the end of the lunar month (you can find out when this is from a moon calendar or from the internet).

- Sit quietly and write down everything from your past that has hurt or disappointed you – everything that didn't go as you would have wished and that you would like to let go of, especially if you can't stop thinking of it or are obsessed with it.

- That night, go out into the garden (if you live in a flat, use an open window or a balcony) and burn what you have written, saying, 'I'm releasing you. Goodbye!'

- Then take another sheet of paper and write down everything you want to invite into your life – exactly how you want things to be in the future, what you are going to bring about and which direction you will take. Make a photocopy of it. Put the copy in an envelope, keep it safely somewhere in your house and do not open it for seven years. That will give time for the energy to mature and all your requests to be understood. People often think that things will change immediately, but that isn't usually how it happens. The universe may have to make many changes to lead you to your heart's desire, so have patience. You will be able to observe the changes as you go along. But if you make up your mind about what you want, your soul will lead the way.

- Wait until the first three days of the new moon then go outside again one night and burn the original piece of paper, saying, 'Bring me all this prosperity. This is what I want – guide me.' This way the energy of the new moon will help your wishes to grow and you will start feeling happy as your soul takes the lead. When you suddenly feel happy you will know you are in touch with your soul.

In this exercise you have started working with the energy of Heaven. When you have completed it, you will notice that 'coincidences' start happening in your life (although of course they are nothing of the kind). You will meet unexpected people, money will come from unexpected places, things will start happening in your job – a thousand tiny miracles will come your way.

If your life needs major change, however, it is normal to find things going wrong all around you after this exercise. Don't worry – this is your soul trying to show you the areas that aren't working in your life, the areas you need to address. See anything negative as a blessing from Heaven. There may be a stage where you feel a bit overwhelmed, but always remember that you are willing to change and that change will be for the better. Focus on the solutions and you will deal with the challenges with greater ease.

The results of this exercise will depend on how honest you were about your intentions, which must come from both your head and your heart. There is only one way to fail, however, and that is if you don't try because you are scared of disappointment. Fear sometimes comes from thinking that nothing will change. But, as my father told me, 'Nothing ventured, nothing gained.' Just keep in mind that the future will be different and always focus on the light at the end of the tunnel – something I have heard from many mediums in different churches. Celebrate your achievements as you go along and be grateful for them.

To make this exercise more effective, you can burn some sage and pass it around your house, opening the windows and doors to let the smoke out. This way you get the Earth energy moving, too. You will fall in love with your house after this exercise!

Here is another exercise that will help you as you take your first steps on the path to creating luck. Remember that we are all unique and each of our lives is like a book. Now's the time to start writing your very own success story:

- Buy a beautiful, good-quality journal and begin writing the story of your life from birth onwards. It really helps to look at a picture of yourself at each life stage, as this will refresh your memory.

- Focus on your needs at the time and your observations now about the way you acted then. To learn from this journal you need to focus on what you would do differently if the situation came up today.

- As your story unfolds you will start seeing the patterns you have followed in life. When you start seeing these patterns and digesting the experiences you have had, keep in mind that they are neither good nor bad. Don't judge them, just look at your actions and emotions with a positive mindset then use your new understanding to shape a happier, healthier future.

- It's not the experiences themselves that are important, but the way you reacted to those experiences.

- At the end of each chapter write what you want to be able to release from that experience and what you want now. It has to be something that will make you feel so happy that the past won't matter!

- Make a deal with your soul that if you get your wish, it will make you feel that you have truly laid the past to rest, learned from it and moved on.

This exercise can be challenging and sometimes painful, but it's worth it, because the insights can be profound – and life-changing.

CHAPTER 4

THE DIRECTIONS OF YOUR HOME

Now you have done your preparation, it's time to familiarize yourself with the directions of your home. Some people use their phones to determine these, while others use the sun. These are valid methods, though I recommend you purchase a good-quality compass. The more accurately you can measure the directions, the better.

First find the centre of your home. You can do this by measuring it back to front and side to side simply by placing your feet in front of each other and counting how many feet there are. Once you have done that, divide it by two and you will have the centre.

Stand in the centre and look to the front of the house, holding your compass in both hands. That way you will be able to establish the directions of your home.

The Meanings of the Directions

According to feng shui, each direction has a meaning. These are based on the trigrams of the *I Ching*, the Chinese 'Book of Changes'.

Here are the meanings for each direction in the home according to hemisphere:

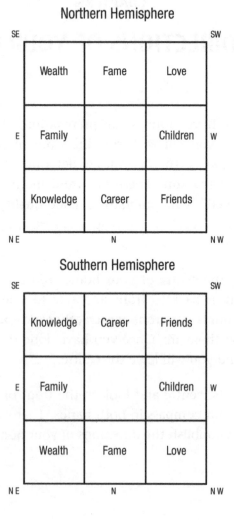

Northern Hemisphere

Wealth	Fame	Love
Family		Children
Knowledge	Career	Friends

Southern Hemisphere

Knowledge	Career	Friends
Family		Children
Wealth	Fame	Love

You will find it really helpful to draw up a plan of your home and mark out where each area is located. Do the same for your workplace.

If you balance your Earth, Human and Heaven energies in each sector you will have great results.

Missing Areas

You may find that your property doesn't conform to a square or rectangular shape and has a missing area.

Floorplan showing missing area

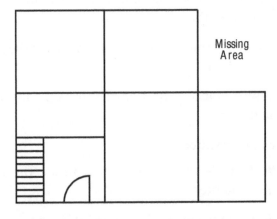

The directions also relate to the people in the home and when an area is missing, whether inside or outside the home, it means that a person will not benefit from or be affected by the energy of the direction. Often this family member is simply not present, perhaps because they have left home. The people and directions are:

Northern Hemisphere

- *North:* Outside the home: mother; inside the home: second son

- *Northeast:* Outside the home: first son; inside the home: third son

- *East:* Outside the home: second daughter; inside the home: first son

- *Southeast:* Outside the home: third daughter; inside the home: first daughter

- *South:* Outside the home: father; inside the home: second daughter

- *Southwest:* Outside the home: first daughter; inside the home: mother

- *West:* Outside the home: second son; inside the home: third daughter

- *Northwest:* Outside the home: third son; inside the home father

Southern Hemisphere

- *North:* Outside the home: father; inside the home: second daughter

- *Northeast:* Outside the home: third daughter; inside the home: first daughter

- *East:* Outside the home: second daughter; inside the home: first son

- *Southeast:* Outside the home: first son; inside the home: third son

- *South:* Outside the home: mother; inside the home: second son

- *Southwest:* Outside the home: third son; inside the home father

- *West:* Outside the home: second son; inside the home: third daughter

- *Northwest:* Outside the home: first daughter; inside the home: mother

If you live in a home that has your own area missing, you might not feel supported in that home.

Your Personal Lucky and Unlucky Directions

As well as the directions of your home, you also have personal lucky and unlucky directions according to your year of birth. This is what is known as the Eight Mansions system. To find your personal directions:

- First find your Ming-gua number (pages 195–6).

- Then check the tables (pages 197–8) to determine whether you are an east or a west person. There are four lucky directions and four unlucky directions for each.

Lucky Personal Directions
Sheng Chi: *Wealth*

This is the most auspicious direction. It brings wealth, recognition, power and authority. In the home it is good if this area is a bedroom or an office. Preferably it should be the place where you spend a lot of time in the day.

Tien Yi: *Doctor from Heaven*

This direction relates to health. It helps to balance this area if you are having money problems. It is helpful to people in a management position and in a manufacturing company it could be the production-line area.

Yen Nien: *Longevity*

This is the direction for peace. It is important to have peace within. If you don't feel good within yourself, balance this direction. It will also help with your love life and relationships at work and home.

Fu Wei: *Control of Life*

This is the direction in which to place your bed if possible. It will help with your career and bring an energy that is calm, so will provide you with long-term clear vision at work.

Unlucky Personal Directions

These directions must be 'supported' by placing objects there that have the energy of the controlling elements (see pages 197–8). This will clear the unlucky energies.

Huo Hai: *Unlucky*

This direction can cause issues with court cases and loss of money. It can bring material worries and make people argumentative. If you have children and find yourself arguing with them, you must declutter this area and keep it tidy. Support this direction by placing wood objects there.

Wu Kwei: *Spiritual Challenges*

Balance this direction if your business is losing money, people aren't nice to you and there is any likelihood of fire in your property. Introduce a lot of light and clean windows. If you find yourself disagreeing with people quite often or feel picked on, check what is happening in this direction of your home. Support this direction by placing earth objects there.

Liu Sha: *Betrayal*

Balance this direction if you are missing opportunities, feeling drained and having arguments and/or small accidents. This area also relates to being sexually betrayed. Support this direction by placing wood objects there.

Chueg Ming: *Life Disasters*

When things go very wrong in any area of your life, make sure this direction is clean and tidy. You can neutralize the energy of this direction by placing water objects there as long as it is not a bedroom. If it is, just make sure is clear of any type of mess.

The Energy of Your Home

Just as each person is either an east or west person, based on the year of their birth, so every property has either east or west energy. This is not based on the year of construction, but on the direction the property faces. If it faces southeast, south, north or east, it is an east house, and if it faces northeast, west, northwest or southwest, it is a west house.

You can create luck much more easily when you live in a property that matches your energy. So, if you are an east person, live in an east house, and if you are a west person live in a west house. If you are part of a family, choose a house according to the breadwinner's direction and it will support all the family and ultimately bring luck to all.

However, if you can't live in a house that matches your energy, all is not lost: if you balance the three energies in your best and worst directions, you can still generate luck!

The Elements

It is important when you start creating luck to look into the balance between the elements relative to the directions. Each direction corresponds to an element and that element will either help you or drain you.

It is important not to have a clash of elements. As an example, metal in the wood direction creates a clash and that is not good. When you are placing furniture, for example, always aim to use elements that nourish the direction. The list below shows you which elements will help which directions.

To get the energy flowing you don't need to use the element of the direction itself, because that energy is already there; instead, use an element that will be supportive and nourishing.

Supportive Elements

Northern Hemisphere

- *Water* is located to the north; nourished by metal

- *Earth* to the northeast and southwest; nourished by fire

- *Wood* to the east and southeast; nourished by water

- *Fire* to the south; nourished by wood

- *Metal* to the west and northwest; nourished by earth

Southern Hemisphere

- *Water* is located to the south; nourished by metal

- *Metal* to the west and southwest; nourished by earth

- *Earth* to the northwest and southeast; nourished by fire

- *Fire* to the north; nourished by wood

- *Wood* to the east and northeast; nourished by water

I recommend that you place in your lucky and unlucky directions the elements for those particular directions. See the list below for suggestions.

When you are placing an element, be creative and remember that whatever you energize will work, because energy follows intention. Use your good taste to make whatever you place look good and match the interior of your home. If whatever you place doesn't look good and makes you feel uncomfortable, it isn't right. On the other hand, if you like your transformation, it is already working.

Some examples of what to use:

- *Wood:* Plants; wooden floors; wooden artwork; the colour green; bamboo; the money plant, or jade plant, as it is called

- *Fire:* The colours red, pink and purple; fire-shaped artwork that has no definition but rises upwards; red carpets or curtains

- *Earth:* Earthy colours, yellows and browns; plant pots; ceramic floors; terracotta vases

- *Metal:* The colours white and grey; granite; metal objects; computers; tables made of metal and glass; white materials; round-shaped cushions; silver artwork

- *Water:* Black and all dark tones of blue (not sky blue); water fountains; aquariums

I find it useful when you work with colours to be aware of their effect on human psychology and behaviour. Bright colours make us happy and we should use them in the active areas of the home, and dark colours make us slow down, so we should use them in the rest areas of the property. Dark colours are yin and bright colours are yang, so a good balance between them is advised.

I like my properties to have just one colour as a canvas. I like to use an earthy pastel tone – the home carries earth energy – so I always choose an earthy colour mixed with white. After that I energize each area with the element required for that direction.

Elemental Cycles

The elements also work either together or against each other in productive or controlling cycles:

DESTRUCTIVE

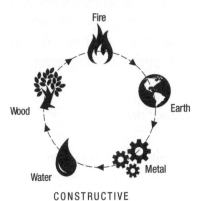

CONSTRUCTIVE

You can use these cycles to balance the directions. For example, if you place a water element, say a fountain, in the wood direction, this will make the wood grow and restore balance.

You can also maximize your luck by creating a productive cycle. In the northern hemisphere, for example, the southeast corresponds to wealth and prosperity and the elements in this direction are earth and wood, so placing the water element in this direction means that the water will feed the wood and create wealth.

The Animals of the Chinese Horoscope

Something else to bear in mind when considering the directions of your home is the Chinese horoscope. Check the tables with the 12 animals (see page 201) to find out which animal you are.

Just like the elements, the animals can have a good relationship with each other or clash with each other (see page 202). Each animal represents an element. If the element of another animal/person feeds your element, you are a good match; if it clashes with your element, you should avoid that type of animal/person.

Animals and Directions

Each animal sign also has a direction:

Northern Hemisphere

- *North:* Rat

- *Northeast:* Ox and tiger

- *East:* Rabbit

- *Southeast:* Dragon and snake

- *South:* Horse

- *Southwest:* Goat and monkey

- *West:* Rooster

- *Northwest:* Dog and pig

Southern Hemisphere

- *North:* Snake

- *Northeast:* Horse and goat

- *East:* Monkey

- *Southeast:* Rooster and dog

- *South:* Pig

- *Southwest:* Rat and ox

- *West:* Tiger

- *Northwest:* Rabbit and dragon

It is auspicious when creating luck to face one of your lucky personal directions and if you can combine this with facing the direction of your animal sign, it will give you a double chance of fame and success.

CHAPTER 5

CAREER

- *Element:* Water

- *Direction:* Northern hemisphere: north; southern hemisphere: south

- *Animal:* Northern hemisphere: rat; southern hemisphere: pig

- *Parts of the Body:* Ears, blood, kidneys, reproductive organs, sexual organs, stomach

- *Members of the Family:* Mother outside the home; second son inside the home

- *Imbalance:* An excess of earth items in this area causes an imbalance, as the earth blocks the way for the water.

- *Solution:* Use water as the main solution and metal as the second solution to activate the energy in this area.

Everyone wants a good career – that's a given. And, unless you are independently wealthy or born with movie-star looks, you will have to work hard to achieve what you want and all that follows: comfort, a nice home, being able to feel financially secure and provide for your family.

The earliest influences on what type of career we choose – whether we follow a creative path or hard-nosed financial one, for example – are our parents, our culture and our tribe. Our family, especially, has a huge influence on us, because they want to mould us, to help us be the best we can be.

Sadly, many of us choose careers for the wrong reasons, for example simply to please our family, and end up doing something that doesn't fulfil us for 50 per cent of our waking hours. This is a tragedy. If you take no pleasure in what you do, you're killing yourself slowly but surely, and probably your career as well. To be successful in your career you must love it. 'Do what you love and the money will follow', as the saying goes. This is because respecting your passion, your dreams, links you to Heaven energy. So, follow your dreams. This needn't mean giving your present career up – use it to pay for your passion until you become independent enough to do just what you want. Start your passion as a hobby if necessary, and be grateful for the job that you don't want to do because it will pay for what you do want to do.

So, start by looking at the career direction of your home. What do you have on the walls? How is the furniture arranged? Is it blocking the flow of energy? Sometimes we place furniture in such a way that we have to go around it to get to the other rooms of our house, and if we have to go around obstacles to get to our career direction it means we will find it hard to achieve career success. So take a good look and think, 'How can I change it? How can I make this career area work for me?'

To do this, first sit quietly and make a list of pros and cons. It's very important to focus like this, because from that moment on you can concentrate on changing the negatives on that list. Remember to focus on solutions.

Your career area must reflect you as a professional or how you would like to be seen as a professional. For example, if you are a writer, the wall should be lined with books to inspire you. Or you could hang a picture there that inspires you, and gives you energy and creativity.

One point I want to make is that you should always use your common sense when making changes. Remember that it's very important for the space we live in to be comfortable and calm. Any environment that is cluttered or chaotic will produce stress and eventually illness. There are many styles of feng shui, some of which involve a great deal of superstition and can make the interior of a property look messy. This cannot be good feng shui. In fact, the best feng shui is virtually invisible, because it blends perfectly with the interior design of a home. If someone has told you that a certain Chinese symbol, say, will bring money flooding in, but that symbol clashes with your culture and the décor of your home, it won't work.

Moving to the outside of your property, the career direction here is important, too. For example, if you gaze out at a cemetery, you will think very spiritual thoughts and may even be drawn to some kind of spiritual career.

To attract prosperity, it's important for the front of your house – which, remember, corresponds to your wealth – to look prosperous. That means keeping the exterior clean and tidy and beautifully painted, with lovely plants and flowers. Then at the back, which relates to your health, take care of yourself by growing organic vegetables, making your garden beautiful and recycling everything you can.

In your office, make sure your future isn't blocked by having your desk facing a wall. The more light in this direction, the more energy you will have to succeed in your career. The rules are that you must always face the main door and have a wall behind you. If you don't have a wall, make sure you have a chair with a back as high as your shoulders when you are seated.

The ideal position for a desk is facing your fame direction (see page 54), as career and reputation go together. One is yin and the other is yang, so they complement each other, and without a good reputation you can't have a good career. If you are having difficulties in your career, the challenge may be in the opposite direction, so check it out. Life must be in balance.

If you are in a management position, it is great for you to face your employees or have your office at the back of the building facing the front. Subconsciously, this means that you are watching your business and are in control.

Whatever you do, be grateful for the job you have. Learn to see your colleagues as souls and respect everyone's dignity. Whatever your position, don't look on yourself as better than others; if you make the people around you feel small, the foundations of success are rotten.

The career direction has a lot to do with taking responsibility and moving forward. A clean desk in this direction means a clean mind. Clearing the clutter will help your energy rise, so don't waste time, get started!

When you are in a large room with many desks, face a direction that brings the energy you are looking for. If you are a manager, for example, face the friends area (see page 54) so that your employees will be helpful.

Wherever you work, bring a picture of your family with you, so you won't forget them and become work-obsessed.

When making changes in your career, you can seek spiritual advice, but be careful how you do this. If you seek it from external sources – a Tarot reading, for example – you are giving your power away. Instead, search for the answers inside. Meditation is very important to me and I recommend that you try it to clarify your thoughts, confront your fears and make decisions.

Whatever you want to do, if you are thinking about starting your own business, you need to keep in mind that it has to be for the good of all. When making a product, make sure it is done with love. If you focus only on the money you can make from it, demand is likely to be short-lived. Aim for quality, too, because that takes creativity, and that brings Heaven energy into the equation, so generates success.

When looking to recruit staff, make sure that you involve them in the business. If you are all working together with one aim, you can create a fantastic product. Generosity with your staff will also bring rewards. If they are overworked and under-rewarded, they will end up sick, your turnover will fall and you will lose money. On the other hand, every company that treats its staff fairly creates good karma for the product, because it carries good energy and makes purchasers feel good also.

Our horoscope also affects our career. The year we were born will be ruled by one of the elements (you can find this out from a Chinese calendar or by coming to the *Creating Luck* workshops). This determines which elements will nourish us and which won't on a more personal level. It is used when drawing up a Chinese astrology chart. It also means we can use feng shui for that selection to determine which day of the month is the most auspicious to start or sell a business, move offices, employ new staff or change jobs.

Recently I worked with the owner of a private bank in London, applying feng shui to his home. He was so impressed that he asked me to help him choose a new team to work with him. Based on his element, we chose 30 applicants. He whittled these down to 10 interviewees and then selected four whose elements were most constructive when combined with his. Guess what? The new team was fantastic and he managed to hit his targets in half the time he had expected.

In this case, the change was extremely rapid, but remember that change that comes through feng shui is usually a gradual process. Energy needs to mature and get settled. I always advise that it may take up to 18 months for changes to happen. That depends how drastic the change is, but you need the foundations to be good in order to make lasting changes in any area of your life, so patience is a good quality to develop along the way.

This is a lovely exercise to invoke Heaven energy to give your inspiration and guidance for your career. It should be done during the new moon, because that's the perfect time for things to begin. It should also be done between 11 p.m. and 5 a.m., because that's the time of Heaven, when we're asleep and our spirit leaves our body.

1. Take a large piece of paper and draw two circles one above the other, overlapping in the middle.

2. Place a white candle in that middle section (it's important it is white, because white means purity of intentions and wishes).

3. In the top circle, write as much detail as you can about the kind of career you would like – the more detail, the better.

4. In the lower circle, write your fears and what is stopping you from moving on.

5. When you've finished, light the candle and make a wish to change your career.

6. Now take the paper and burn it in the flame of the white candle. The smoke will evaporate up into Heaven and you will be firmly telling your subconscious to bring you the job you are looking to find. If you're doing this inside, please be careful when the candle burns down. You should let it burn all the way to the end and preferably not blow it out, as if you do that you will find the wax of the candle spreads everywhere. If it does that anyway when you burn the candle to the end, it is because there was a lot to clear, but if the candle burns nicely to the end it means the energy has been totally accepted and the change you asking for is likely to proceed smoothly, too.

You will find that this exercise is very powerful, and the more honest you can be, the deeper the effects. You are activating that super-computer inside your skull, telling it what you want and using Earth and Heaven energy to achieve it.

After this exercise, remain alert: coincidences will happen, the right vacancy will be advertised or someone will tell you about a job. Wait and see!

CHAPTER 6

SPIRITUALITY AND KNOWLEDGE

- *Element:* Earth

- *Direction:* Northern hemisphere: northeast; southern hemisphere: southeast

- *Animal:* Northern hemisphere: ox and tiger; southern hemisphere: dog and rooster

- *Parts of the Body:* Hands, back, shoulders, feet, legs

- *Members of the Family:* First son outside the home; third son inside the home

- *Imbalance:* An excess of wood items in this area causes an imbalance, as the wood drains the earth.

- *Solution:* Use earth as the main solution and fire as the second solution to activate the energy in this area.

Now let's explore the direction of spirituality. Spirituality plays a fundamental part in who we are and want to be, so it's essential that we get in touch with this side of ourselves at some point in our lives.

If your property faces in this direction, or the opposite direction, it will have a certain energy. This often includes an excess of earth in the middle of the property, so this type of home usually needs an important cure.

If you live in home facing the spirituality direction, you need to introduce fire at the front. That will protect your home against any negative spiritual influences that might attack it. In China, this famous cure involves painting the front door red. This immediately attracts the right energy. It's amazingly powerful – people's lives can take off after a simple coat of paint. The fire energy helps people to be in tune with their spirituality and you often find people living in these types of properties are very religious.

What I observed once in Beijing was a road full of restaurants with red doors. They were all facing northeast and all busy with customers. I asked Great Grand Master Chan about it and he explained to me that earth energy relates to food, in this case spiritual food, and that's why people were enjoying eating in these restaurants.

Properties facing the spirituality direction are extremely powerful places to live in, because the relationship with Heaven energy is so strong. This can either make us or break us, because Heaven energy has complete power over Earth energy. These two powerful forces are meant to work together, with humans somewhere in the middle.

Whichever way your house faces, if you are an artist or a writer and need inspiration, you should pay special attention to the spirituality area of your property. Build a small altar there for devotion or meditation – that part of your home should be a place for peace and quiet, for reflection.

These rooms are also very good for sleeping in, because when we sleep we dream, so we are in a perfectly receptive state of mind. People who live in properties facing the spirituality direction do tend to dream a lot, although they are often still weary when they wake, because their dreams are really spiritual journeys.

Another thing I've found is that these properties can be very tough on the women who live there. They often end up with some kind of illness, so I tell people to paint the interior white to get all of the earth stress out of the house. Your mind, body and spirit must be at peace for you to be healthy.

I mentioned fire energy earlier. It's important to introduce it into these houses for protection. There are many ways to do so, such as placing red pots in front of your house or lighting a candle in the window at night. That energy will protect you and create the inner peace that we all crave. I have known people who have complained of seeing spirits in unguarded homes.

This type of property also needs to be cleansed at regular intervals, so every three months burn some pure sage in every room. This will help get the energy moving, because it tends to stagnate in these houses.

In the back, you should always have a water fountain running to keep the wood energy moving. If you are a woman who is having trouble finding a husband, introduce more wood energy into the home to bring love into your life. Buy some lovely plants and place them in the middle of the house, or have a beautiful display of cut flowers in a vase. You could also introduce a permanent fixture that represents wood – perhaps a statue carved from wood or wooden shelving.

It's funny, but my speciality has been properties facing the spirituality direction. I have created good feng shui in many of these homes over the years. For example, I was recently called to a road in London where all the houses faced northeast. I worked on three houses there and found very similar issues in each. They were all grand five-storey properties and the men living there were all very wealthy. Curiously enough, some of the wealthiest clients I have had have lived in northeast-facing properties. In this case, the men had all done very well in their chosen careers but, because of the earth stress present in their homes, they weren't very good listeners and argued terribly with their wives. For their part, the women were all very harassed, with lots of kids running around.

Most of my work in those homes was in the gardens. I introduced red vases beside the paths and beautiful red flowers like peonies – I often use peonies because they carry a loving energy into the home. When they bloom people can't help but feel calm and happy, and that energy is transmitted into the household. I also painted the interiors of two of these houses white, to counteract the earth energy. And because the properties were so messy and chaotic we did a major decluttering and brought metal energy into the rooms we couldn't paint. Metal energy helps to drain excess earth energy.

Over the course of a year the couples stopped arguing, started respecting each other more and the husbands listened much more carefully. One of the couples was divorcing when I gave them the consultation, but they are still together now. Of course, those changes weren't all down to feng shui – the couples worked hard to improve their relationships, too. And the intention to change was already present, otherwise they wouldn't have contacted me. But the feng shui certainly helped, especially adding beautiful feminine flowers on the right-hand side of the house to support the wives and more masculine plants and flowers on the left-hand side to help the husbands.

If you are moving to a property facing the spirituality direction, please seek the help of a feng shui consultant. Spiritual people tend to love this type of property, but not everyone can handle it.

In the northern hemisphere, northeast-facing churches are very common and it seems to me that our ancestors knew something about energy flow. Many of the churches are wealthy, too.

Personally, the spirituality direction will connect you to Heaven energy, help you to obtain your heart's desires and strengthen your intuition. We all have intuition, but most of us are afraid to follow it. That could jeopardize the life we have built up for ourselves, so we ignore it. But sooner or later we all have to face our soul.

Here are some suggestions to help you to connect to Heaven energy:

- The best way to forge a relationship with your spiritual side is to try a range of approaches to see which works best for you – yoga, meditation or simply going for a walk by yourself in a beautiful park can all help. As you walk, ask yourself questions about your life. Explore where you have come from, where you are now and where you would like to be a year from now. When you start asking yourself these questions, answers will percolate up from your subconscious mind.

- If you can meditate, even better. It doesn't need to be for long – just 20 minutes a day can be tremendously powerful. If you clear your mind and sit in peaceful contemplation for that short time, guidance will come to you. I believe that when we open up in this way, we connect to the spirit inside us.

- You can also try lying on the floor for 10 minutes and thinking about the present and the future. It works especially well if you do it in the spirituality direction of your home and even better outside in the garden at night, looking at the stars.

CHAPTER 7

FAMILY

- *Element:* Wood

- *Direction:* Northern hemisphere: east; southern hemisphere: east

- *Animal:* Northern hemisphere: rabbit; southern hemisphere: monkey

- *Parts of the Body:* Liver, gallbladder, joints, feet, legs, eyes, heart

- *Members of the Family:* Second daughter outside the home; first son inside the home

- *Imbalance:* An excess of metal items in this area causes an imbalance, as the metal chops the water.

- *Solution:* Use wood as the main solution and water as the second solution to activate the energy in this area.

Whether we are in the northern or southern hemisphere, the east is all to do with our families, especially our relationship with our elders – our parents, grandparents or the people who brought us up, as well as our ancestors who have passed to the spirit world. They planted the seed from which we grew. We are inextricably linked to them, both physically and spiritually, because they gave us life.

What's interesting is that to be truly successful, we need to have a very good relationship with our elders. As we've seen already, it's especially important to have a good relationship with our parents. Remember that whatever they wish for us is what we are likely to become.

This family direction can be complemented with pictures of your ancestors or an altar for them. Make it beautiful with candles and flowers and just ask for help because your ancestors aren't far away and it won't be long before you get an answer.

If you feel things stagnating, sometimes blasting the stereo in this direction can be very helpful. It does move energy around.

When you use these energies for business it can be very interesting because the type of clients you will attract will be family-oriented and fun.

A long time ago I was asked to help design a shopping mall in Playa del Carmen, Mexico. There were to be many different kinds of shops and other attractions and I had to place the buildings in directions that would help the mall to thrive. Then I had a fantastic idea: why not put a nightclub in the east, so the thunderous noise and energy would breathe life into the whole mall? So a building on the east side was rented out to a club, and a gym was also located in that direction – gyms are also all about movement, growth and energy. Because this gym had high-tempo music in the background while people were exercising, we generated even more positive energy.

We were also very careful to build the mall in an environmentally sustainable way and make sure it worked in harmony with the surrounding landscape. The land we built it on had a lot of history and a number of old buildings, which we kept, and we performed a ceremony before the building began, asking Mother Nature for permission to build there. We kept every single tree that was over 50 years old and didn't touch anything on the land that would have been inappropriate.

The mall's mouth was to the sea and its tail faced the city. We used the urban energy that flowed from a road leading from the city into the heart of the mall. On the mall's north side we placed a water symbol, with softly flowing waters, while the south was open, with a fantastic view of a huge fountain, which shot great jets of water into the sky. That mall has been a massive success. It's busy all the time, full of locals every weekend and tourists throughout the year.

So what do you need to think about if you live in an east-facing property? I always check what's happening in the middle. One thing to look out for is whether you have a toilet there. People who live in east-facing properties often make a lot of money, but if they have a toilet or spiral staircase in the middle, that money will slip away.

Whichever way your property is facing, a key issue to look at is whether the east is missing. If you have a gap there, your relationship with your ancestors is unhealthy. If that gap is on the inside, it will affect your eldest son. If it's on the outside, your second daughter will suffer. They will feel unsupported and alone in the world, but feng shui can be used to support them and give them a sense of belonging. You may also find that an internal gap causes problems with your eyes, heart and head, while an external gap affects your feet, legs and freedom of movement.

If you are having problems with your parents or unresolved issues with those who have passed away, you need to take action to transform this. Start by hanging pictures of your elders on the east-facing wall of your home. That way you will bring those family members into your life, which will help cure any communication problems you are having. Put up a shelf and line it with photos of your parents, grandparents and even great-grandparents if you can find them. All these wise elders will guide you through your life and your relationships with those still living will blossom, which is one of the most important things for our mental and emotional well-being.

Ask for guidance from your ancestors and be grateful for them, because they will help you to open many doors. When you talk to the spirit world you must remember to be focused and explain exactly what you are trying to achieve. Also remember that there is no time in the spirit world, so patience may be needed. If you are focused, your loved ones will understand what you need, but give them time to help you with it.

The family direction can also be good for our health. If someone is ill, the energy in this direction can bring them more vitality.

Here is an exercise for the family area:

1. If you enjoy a good relationship with your parents, write down everything you are grateful for in that relationship. This gratitude will, in turn, strengthen the bond.

2. If your relationship with your parents is more challenging, start by writing down everything you want to forgive yourself for – all the mistakes and wrong turns you have made in the past. Then write down everything you would like to forgive your parents for – all the harsh words or times when you felt they didn't support you, especially during your adolescence. Remember that during adolescence it is fairly normal to hate our parents, but this is just a hormonal time and will pass eventually.

(This part of the exercise can be difficult, because we are often so attached to anger and blame that it's hard to let go and forgive. But trust me, it will become easier as you continue and in the end you will forgive yourself and your parents. This is one of the most healing gifts we can give ourselves.

As I mentioned earlier, many people find it difficult to have a good relationship with their parents because they haven't decided to take responsibility for their own lives and they blame their parents for where they are. But if you are on the path to creating luck, you must move on from this.)

3. Next, think about the language your parents use when speaking to or about you. Identify the negative words, phrases and descriptions they use and start training them to speak more positively about you. Remind them that negativity profoundly affects your confidence and self-esteem. No parent wants to hurt their child so, slowly, you will reprogram them to give you the loving energy you need and deserve.

4. Go back to step 1 and write down everything that you are grateful for about your new relationship with your parents.

CHAPTER 8

WEALTH

- *Element:* Earth

- *Direction:* Northern hemisphere: southeast; southern hemisphere: northeast

- *Animal:* Northern hemisphere: dragon and snake; southern hemisphere: horse and goat

- *Parts of the Body:* Nerves, thighs, posterior, hips, waist, mouth

- *Members of the Family:* Third daughter outside the home; first daughter inside the home

- *Imbalance:* An excess of metal items in this area causes an imbalance, as the metal drains the earth.

- *Solution:* Use wood as the main solution and water as the second solution to activate the energy in this area.

One of the most common enquiries I get is how to generate material wealth. Everyone (unless they are Bill Gates or Warren Buffett) needs more money, right?

Let's learn the basic principle right at the start: if we want to be wealthy and prosperous, we must be thankful for what we have every day. That way we will activate Heaven energy. The more we thank the soul inside us, the more we will have.

The first thing I do when I'm called out to a house is to check the front door. You can tell immediately whether a property can generate money for the occupants by the front door. Often it can't, but if it does contain untapped wealth, you often just need to re-hang the door so that it is oriented to a specific direction to access the money. Any feng shui consultant from the Chue Foundation can help you with that.

Moving on to how to become wealthy, you attract wealth by being generous in your heart and soul. Anyone, no matter how rich or poor, can do it. But do you believe that you truly deserve wealth? That is the question. You can only create money luck if you do believe you deserve it. Then, feel as if you already have it – that activates the belief.

I do believe that if you seek you shall find, as long as you use the power of your will for your own benefit financially without harming or taking advantage of others.

Focus is key. I use Louise Hay's affirmations; I place them everywhere. My favourite for material success is

'Money comes to me easily.' The affirmations help me to stay focused.

If you have been traumatized by hardship and poverty, you must use the exercises in this book to break the patterns. Prosperity is possible and if you believe you deserve the best, you will achieve it, but it starts with drawing on your Heaven energy and programming your thoughts.

My friends used to say to me that I was too positive for them. This hurt my feelings, but didn't divert me from my belief in being positive. If you are having a bad time with money, be positive and focus on the solution. Then act – don't stagnate with the shame or embarrassment of having made financial mistakes.

The other day I watched a TV programme about a couple working through their financial problems together and it was very inspiring, because the husband had hidden his troubles from his wife until his debts were such that he had to come clean. Then, to his surprise, his wife declared that she was supporting him, because she knew in her heart that he had only got into debt because he wanted the best for the family.

If you are in a similar situation, your loved ones you might not be happy to start with, but your passion to make things better will gain their support. The important thing is to be honest about the mess you have made.

If you are the type of person who is in financial difficulties because of continually changing career, focus on your passion. That way you will learn what you truly want. But be responsible, too – it is important to do your current job well and not leave until you are financially stable, especially if you have a family.

However, as we have already discussed, it is important to do what you love. So, if you wake up in the morning and just can't face going to work, you need to go into your heart to find out what you want and then start to make the necessary changes.

Passion is what is important. Focusing solely on financial rewards isn't the way to wealth. If you think that way, you can have the most auspicious feng shui for money there is, but all that will happen will be that you will lose it as quickly as you make it. Instead, focus on creativity and the good of others. That will connect you to your Heaven energy and make things happen for you. If you are a business manager, for example, and you focus on the well-being of your employees rather than on achieving targets just to prove yourself, you have a good chance of making the targets as well as being an excellent manager. My view is that you must bring spirituality to work in order to achieve success.

It's crucial that you desire to make money yourself, too, not inherit it or marry it. Don't sell your soul for money – get out there and earn it. Marrying for the sake of security is just asking for trouble. Marry only for love.

If you want to improve your finances, always focus on being healthy first. That may sound contradictory, but you can't have wealth without health. Also, keep the southeast of your home bright and in order.

I had a client once who was desperate to make money in his shop, but when I arrived and looked at the southeast, I found a stock room there full of boxes. The energy wasn't moving anywhere, as there wasn't even a window. Over the long term I told my client to consider placing a window there, but a short-term remedy was to paint the door dark blue. That door was visible from the entrance of the shop and looked amazing. The coat of paint alone was enough to activate the intention and sales improved immediately.

I have also been to see properties where the occupants were really happy but had no money, and the reason was the shape of the property – the southeast was missing, so the property had no wealth.

So, be grateful for what you already have, take care of your health, keep your southeast area clean and tidy and focus on what you want and you will become wealthy. Simple! But may I remind you that money also brings karma with it. Material success is only enjoyable when you share it and use it to help others.

As you achieve material reward, however, you will naturally feel your heart energy expanding and will in turn become more generous. Generosity doesn't mean looking after people – it means teaching them how to look after themselves. 'Give a man a fish and you feed him for a day. Teach a man to fish and you feed him for a lifetime', as the saying goes. That really applies when it comes to generosity.

Remember to be considerate to others as well and never forget those who helped you in the past. Be grateful for what they have given you and more will come your way. Help even those who weren't nice to you if they ask, as that will create a feeling of gratitude in the core of your heart.

Turning to specific feng shui remedies, if you want to create financial luck, start with the wealth direction. Is it there? If it is missing on the inside, your first daughter will be affected. You may also have problems with your hips and waist. If it's missing externally, the third daughter may experience problems. Of course, if you don't have any daughters, you don't need to worry! But the missing area will still affect your health, usually relating to the mouth.

Do you have heavy furniture in that direction? If so, remember that feng shui is like acupuncture – moving that furniture can release all the trapped energy just like inserting a needle in the body. Something as simple as that can change your whole life.

Another simple thing you can do is to introduce water energy to the wealth direction. If you add a fountain, say, in this part of your property, you will create movement, and that will activate a whole host of positive financial changes your life. Once a month, however, there is a bad day for placing a fountain there. It is called a 'sat' day. A

Chue consultant will be able to work out the best date to make your venture successful.

You could also use a glass vase filled with water, and if you add flowers too, you will definitely generate positive energy.

Be careful, though: water can weaken you and make you ill if placed in the wrong part of your property. For example if your bedroom is in the southeast, you can't place water there because you will become unwell.

One place I often put a water feature is diagonally opposite the entrance to the living room. That's where people's money area is often located.

Also try placing a light in the wealth direction, always facing upwards to generate positive energy. And make sure the windows are clean, so that good energy can come pouring in.

If you're unsure, always consult a Chue consultant to make sure you use elements that will make you stronger, not weaker.

I have often found that houses with a nearby church facing towards the wealth area can have a problem with money. Too much religious energy causes the stagnation of money.

Let me give you an example of how powerful this area can be. I once worked with a young man who had been taking drugs and had a really bad reputation. His mother asked me to help him.

When I visited his house, it was on a cliff. Nothing that this man had tried, career-wise, had worked, and it was no surprise to me, because the wealth area was missing from his house. The property was L-shaped, so that vitally important direction simply did not exist. When I started working with him I got him to move out of that house, in fact to a completely different city.

I also did some spiritual healing and counselling with him, so we could change his patterns of belief and behaviour and bring more Heaven energy in to fortify his soul. Coaching him in this way brought in both Human and Heaven energy.

Once we got him into the new house, we brought in Earth energy too and everything changed. We activated his creativity by keeping his house simple and uncluttered but full of his favourite things, plus beautiful artwork and lovely furniture. Almost overnight, the young man stopped drinking and taking drugs. He became really interested in health and started doing yoga and working with a life coach so he could change the interior of his brain as well as the interior of his property. He became interested in property development and is now happy, successful and very wealthy, so it's a wonderful story and I'm so pleased to have been able to help him.

You material wealth can not only be affected by your home, but also by the feng shui of the city you live in. Many towns and cities around the world are auspiciously placed for material riches. Take Geneva: its lake is shaped like a money bag, which is why you find so much money there. Singapore was actually designed to be shaped like a money bag, which of course brought capital flooding in. But recently they made a serious error, because they built a bridge across the financial district and that cut the flow of money and resulted in a major financial crash. How did they solve the problem? Simply by moving a fountain from one side of that bridge to the other, so the money energy could flow freely again.

In Singapore, the one-dollar coin was also designed as a charm for the population to carry in their wallets, so they would always have money. The design of the whole city has been approved by feng shui masters who work just for the council, and when you are there you can enjoy a feng shui tour and appreciate one of the most amazing cities in the world.

Other cities gaining financially from their feng shui include Monaco, Nice and Rio de Janeiro. My master took me to Rio and showed me how the huge statue of Christ looked down over the money-bag shaped bay and the wealthiest, most prosperous areas, while his back protected the more disadvantaged areas, so both parts of Rio. He also pointed out how the Sugar Loaf mountain guarded the bay and protected the city's wealth.

If you would like to use the power of the wealth direction to generate more money in your life, there are some simple but hugely powerful exercises you can try:

- One of the best ways to unlock the money in your home is to create a wish wall in the wealth area. On this wall you should hang a cork board covered in everything you want to bring into your life – the man or woman you want to marry, the home you want to live in, the logo of clients you want to win or the company you hope to work for... Everything that means wealth to you should go on this wall, so every time you look at it you are programming your brain to go after those things you want and deserve. Just make sure they are things you really need.

- Another fantastic exercise, especially if you are in financial difficulties and really need money, is to photocopy the highest-denomination note of your country. Copy one side of that note and then put it in your wallet, around your home, in your car, at work, wherever you want. The more you see money, the more you program your brain to use your talents and creativity to go out and earn it.

- One more exercise that always works (and one that Jim Carrey did when he was a struggling actor) is to write a cheque to yourself for the amount you want in your bank account. So make out a cheque to yourself for a million pounds, or a million dollars, payable to you, then keep it in your wallet. You will find, just like Jim Carrey, that the money eventually comes to you.

Money is the easiest part of life. That is my belief. The day you truly believe this statement it will be true for you also. Develop respect for money and value it as you earn it, but mainly get in touch with your Heaven energy, as if you are looking to create financial security, the real help will come from your soul.

CHAPTER 9

INSPIRATION, REPUTATION AND FAME

- *Element:* Fire

- *Direction:* Northern hemisphere: south; southern hemisphere: north

- *Animal:* Northern hemisphere: horse; southern hemisphere: snake

- *Parts of the Body:* Heart, eyes, small intestine, head

- *Members of the Family:* Father outside the home; second daughter inside the home

- *Imbalance:* An excess of water items in this area causes an imbalance, as the water puts out the fire.

- *Solution:* Use fire as the main solution and wood as the second solution to activate the energy in this area.

This is my favourite direction because it governs inspiration, creativity, illumination, reputation and fame. As it connects to the career direction, because they are opposing directions on the compass, if you have a bad reputation, your career will suffer. Remember that what people think and say about you is very important, because it will spread. The more people talk positively about you, the more positive energy you will create.

Make that your starting-point. Ask yourself: 'What is my image right now? And how is that image affecting my business or home life?' The best way to find this out is to ask people how they see you as a person. That can be an eye-opener! So often we are blind to the image we project.

If people are to think well of you, that means being a good professional, a good father or mother, a good husband or wife, a good friend, a good citizen. Look at the reputation direction of your property and check whether it's too dark, which means your illumination and life energy will be dimmed and you will lack creativity and inspiration. On the other hand, if it's too light – for example if there's a big window there with sunshine streaming through – you will have too much energy and will be overwhelmed by it. People with too much light in this area often have trouble finishing projects, because the energy is too powerful and distracting.

Let me give you an example of the powerful effect this direction can have. I once worked with an extremely talented musician whose second CD was selling really poorly. She couldn't understand it, because her first one had done extremely well. Of course for musicians, artists, actors and any other creative people, reputation is extremely important, so I immediately checked that direction.

She was in the northern hemisphere and her home actually faced south, which was great for her reputation, but she had a river in front of it, which was clashing with the south's fire energy. When fire and water clash, they create smoke, which isn't a bad thing in itself – it creates movement, but that movement is only temporary. So what I needed to do was introduce a lot of wood energy, because wood drinks water and feeds fire. One of the best ways to introduce wood energy is with plants, but always use succulent plants in this area, never spiky ones, because that will create jealousy, with people resenting your fame and good fortune. When we introduced the plants, the musician's reputation was restored and the sales of her CD immediately went up. She was obviously delighted and so was I.

One thing to remember when we're talking about reputation is that people will always gossip about you – that's a natural part of the human condition. Gossip in itself is not a bad thing, but negative gossip is a way of jealousy expressing itself. Instead of provoking jealousy, we have to make sure we create a positive vibe about us in the wider world.

What does this mean in practical terms? For a start, it means projecting the right image. For business, you should make sure your company logo is on the exterior wall of the reputation direction. In the home, use photos that project your desired image to the world. If you want people to see your family as united and strong, hang pictures in this area showing you all together, happy and loving.

As always in feng shui, the garden is vital, too. I was once called to a house in west London, near Heathrow airport. The wife asked me to visit, because her husband was really depressed. He was stuck in his career and was struggling to make ends meet and provide for his family.

When I heard about their problems, I immediately went out to see the garden, which faced south. There was a very beautiful tree growing there, but over the years it had become covered in ivy. The ivy was strangling it and was also creating the shape of a head. As this was in the husband's direction, it was making him depressed and unwell.

First we cut away all the ivy, but the poor tree was too sick to save, so we cut it down. The pressure on the husband disappeared overnight. Totally re-energized, he set up a taxi company which was extremely successful and solved all the family's money worries. That's my favourite kind of feng shui – a small cure with a big effect. It's also an example of how the exterior of a property can be more powerful than the interior when you're dealing with the reputation direction, because it's your link to Heaven energy.

If this area is missing inside the home, the second daughter won't feel supported and may leave home much too early. If the area is missing outside, the father will be affected and may be absent. In terms of health, it will affect the head, causing physical ailments like migraines or psychological difficulties. The eyes, too, can be affected, so make sure the windows are clean in this direction.

If your house is really messy in the reputation direction, beware. You may have a bad reputation, so start sorting it out. People do judge us, especially professionally, so place an image of someone successful there. Create the image of well-being and success will follow.

Here's an exercise focusing on reputation. For most people this means their career and how they are perceived in the workplace, so it concentrates on these areas, but you can make it more general if you wish.

Spend some time thinking about your career – where you are and where you want to be in the future. Then get a pile of magazines and start cutting out pictures of people who do the same job as you but are more famous and successful. If you're in banking, cut out pictures of the top bankers at Goldman Sachs. If you work in property, find pictures of Donald Trump. If you're an actor, cut out pictures of Robert de Niro or Kate Winslet, and so on.

The idea behind this is that if you model yourself on people who have already achieved great success, you will follow in their footsteps. Start researching those people and find out where they went to school, how they got their first break and the path their career followed. Stick their pictures on a cork board and hang it in your reputation area. You are making the statement: 'I want to be like those people. How can I get to where they are?'

You are asking the universe to guide you, and it will. Suddenly you will find many tiny coincidences happening in your life, but of course there is no such thing as coincidence. Heaven energy is guiding you, directing you towards opportunities and people who will help you achieve your goal. At the same time, you are programming your brain, telling it that you want to be famous, materially successful and happy. Just watch: all those things will come to you.

One final point: once you achieve your success, make sure you pay it forward. Give something back to those who are needier than you, perhaps via a charity, because gratitude for your success and generosity to others creates good karma. That gratitude will bring more success, and you will be amazed at how many wonderful things come to you.

CHAPTER 10

LOVE

- *Element:* Earth

- *Direction:* Northern hemisphere: southwest; southern hemisphere: northwest

- *Animal:* Northern hemisphere: goat and monkey; southern hemisphere: dragon and rabbit

- *Parts of the Body:* Digestion, fertility, hips, waist, stomach

- *Members of the Family:* First daughter outside the home; mother inside the home

- *Imbalance:* An excess of wood items in this area causes an imbalance, as the wood drains the earth.

- *Solution:* Use earth as the main solution and fire as the second solution to activate the energy in this area.

When a client calls me because they are having problems with their love life, I always start out in this particular direction and think about what it is portraying. How are the objects organized? For example, if all of them are single, without a matching partner, what is that person unconsciously expressing? So many people think they want love, but in their heart they aren't ready for it. Their property and possessions often reflect that.

If the relationship area of your property is missing completely, unsurprisingly the relationships in your life will be affected. The interior reflects the woman, or wife, so if this is missing there will be no wife in the home. If the northwest in the northern hemisphere and the southwest in the southern hemisphere is missing, there will be no husband. So when I go for a consultation centred around relationships, I'm looking for both those areas and to make a connection between them that will allow the male and female to connect. This is often a problem in apartments, because they tend to be oddly shaped. In houses it's much less of an issue.

Another key point is that when the relationship's direction is missing, people don't have a very satisfying sex life. That's to be expected, of course, because sex is a fundamental part of a loving relationship, or at least it should be.

Sometimes I find people living in a perfectly balanced home where everything seems right but they are still alone. Often it is their astrology that is causing the problem. In that case Jillian Stott will prepare a chart for me and I can then match up the feng shui of the person's home with their personal feng shui to bring love into their life.

At other times, the problem is more obvious. I once did a consultation at a house in the countryside for a couple who were arguing terribly and were totally unable to communicate with each other. When I arrived at the property I immediately visited the garden, which was in the love direction, and found the couple had planted a big spiky tree next to the wall to stop people from climbing over it. They thought they were protecting themselves, but in fact the spikiness of the tree was causing spikiness in their relationship. We removed the tree and within 12 months their relationship had blossomed.

You do have to be careful about what you place in the love direction of your home. Are there any heavy items of furniture that are blocking you from having a relationship? What is hanging on the walls? Think about the poems or pictures you have hanging there, because strange photos or abstract paintings can bring odd words to our mouths. And we have to be very careful what we say in our relationships because words spoken in anger can cause lasting damage.

So, what feng shui can you do to make the most of your property's love direction? If you want to attract someone into your life, your home has to welcome them. Create a balance of male and female energy, so whoever enters you home will feel comfortable there. Women tend to make their home extremely feminine, and tidy and clean, but if we want someone to stay with us, they need to feel relaxed. Men tend to be more laid-back about tidiness and cleanliness, but it's always best to make an effort when bringing a girlfriend home for the first time – first impressions always stay with a person.

Above all, make sure that the love area of your home is organized and in balance. Place things in pairs, so that you program your subconscious to think about sharing, which is the key to a successful relationship, particularly if you have spent a long time by yourself.

Try placing a vase full of water in your relationships area, or water-loving plants like bamboo or peonies. Make sure the windows there are always really clean, because they represent your eyes and the eyes are the window to the soul – if you're going to meet someone, they have to be able to gaze into your eyes.

If you are a woman and you introduce the wood element in this direction – gently, not in excess, maybe through some red flowers, say peonies – you will find a relationship right away.

Before you get carried away, however, think about your intentions. Do you want a relationship because you want something out of it? Or are you going to enjoy the moment whatever happens?

I have encountered a lot of personal agendas when researching love and relationships, including girls and guys who expect a partner to be rich, handsome and look after them and people who hate their lives so much that they feel that it will be better to live someone else's. This sort of thing never works. We have to *become* what we are looking for in a relationship and above all accept ourselves as we are.

I also get clients, mostly girls, who can't understand why they can't find a partner but are victims of their own thinking, because they have an idea of how that partner has to be and anyone who doesn't match up will be rejected. We may seek perfection, but remember that the best relationships are imperfect. We learn from our partners, and experiencing hard times together makes a relationship stronger and teaches us valuable lessons about life and love.

Some people suffer from the 'kangaroo effect' – they jump from one partner to another. What is happening here is these people are very insecure and want to be in control. The moment they lose control, they will detach, as the territory becomes 'unsafe'. The kangaroo effect is likely to result from seeing a parent giving up and moving on in relationships. That pattern is then repeated, due to the fact that the person doesn't understand that for a relationship to work you need to stay with it. Usually they become unfaithful, because they are very insecure. When someone is unfaithful it is always about *them*, not you, so don't let it damage your confidence.

What happens to many single people is that they see sex as love and that is not entirely correct. You can have sex with love in it, but love is something that grows with time and getting to know another person. Basing a relationship on sex is very wrong. A good relationship starts as a friendship first. If you can be friends, you can be together for ever.

So, to find the right partner, you really must spend time with someone. Spend at least a year dating. In that year you will get an idea of what the person is like. Move in together after that and take at least three years to get to know each other. Once the four years are over you will know if it will be for ever or not.

The idea that there is a soul mate out there for us is correct, but soul mates don't always come in the shape of our other half. Our soul mate could be a special person who comes into our life and shows us the way to happiness. That is the true meaning of a soul mate. If it happens to be your lover, all the better.

You can tell what a person is all about by the way they treat you. If they don't respect your boundaries or they try to control you, clearly the relationship is out of balance. And whatever you get before marriage is what you will also get after marriage.

So what should you look for? Character is the most important thing, but an ability to make you laugh is sublime, because it lifts up the soul.

I always advise people who just don't seem to find the right type of person to look for a good psychotherapist, to help them to unblock their emotions. We all need to allow ourselves to be loved. When our hearts are broken, we think that something is wrong with us, but in reality all we need is more courage to be loved.

Being used emotionally and financially and afterwards getting dumped is a common problem. The reason for it is that we are vulnerable and want to be loved, so we try to engage with others and give them the benefit of the doubt. We may end up having a great time, but after a while reality will kick in and the person will turn out to be a liar or a cheat or an alcoholic – some kind of issue always seems to come up.

Nevertheless, people have a hard time letting these sorts of relationships go. At times like these it is important to listen to advice from friends and family. Try counselling, too, or spiritual healing, but whatever you do, start focusing on creating a good relationship, not an exploitative one. Connect with Heaven through your creative thoughts and you will get an answer. There is someone out there for you – every saucepan has a lid to go on it.

Believe you deserve it, check out what your relationships direction is reflecting and make sure you aren't living as a victim. Break the patterns and get out there and meet people, make friends, make a family – whatever you conceive your perfect relationship to be, live it to the full. Life is meant to be shared.

In a relationship, your home provides the Earth energy, sex provides the Human energy and love provides the Heaven energy. Once you fall in love every time you make love, your souls will meet and bond you together.

The relationships area also represents friendship, so if you want to attract more friends you need to pay some attention to it. Think about who you are and what image you project into the world. What do you have to offer people? How can you make yourself more desirable through learning new things, taking up new hobbies, socializing? Also look to develop yourself by thinking about your appearance, your hair and clothes, basically being kind to yourself and treating yourself as well as you want others to treat you. An excellent tactic here is to think of yourself as a brand. What do you have to offer that no one else does? How can you learn to market yourself – your true self, not the person you pretend or want to be?

What might be holding you back? If you have a tendency to control others, you may overstep the boundaries and that makes friendship really hard to maintain. Remember there is a difference between protecting your friends and running their lives for them. Give your opinion, but never make the final decision – let your friends create their own lives. When you respect them as they are, a deeper, more meaningful friendship will develop and you will make many friends.

And if you want something more than friendship, here's my favourite exercise for creating love. It is most effective if you do it at new moon.

1. As you need to set your subconscious mind on a mission to find love for you, be specific in what you tell it, so the first thing to do is to get hold of magazines and cut out pictures of your ideal-looking partner.

2. The next thing is to write down all the qualities you want them to have.

3. Glue all the pictures you have cut out around the list you have written and frame it. Hang it in front of your bed for seven days and make sure you look at it every day.

   (To add power to your mission you can read Psalm 91 every day in front of it. If your religion does not use the Bible, find the relevant prayer for union. Every form of religious practice will have a meaningful prayer. Saying the prayer as part of this exercise attracts good energy relating to your soul.)

4. On the eighth day, take your page from the frame. Wait until evening and then place a white candle on a saucer. Spread honey around it and place a glass of water to the side.

5. Light the candle.

   Read Psalm 91 (or your relevant prayer) again and say, 'As I burn these wishes, the universe will bring the partner I need.'

   Then burn the page, preferably on top of a container that will hold the ashes.

6. Take the ashes, go outside, and let the wind carry them all away. Feel your wishes going out into the universe.

You have to be very specific with the details with this exercise, as one of my clients found out. She asked for a single man who had no baggage and liked to travel. She did get one, but she forgot to add that she wanted him to marry her, so she fell in love with a single guy with no baggage who travelled a lot and took her with him, but he was a sportsman and marriage was not on his agenda.

Love and relationships are important to us all, so I have decided to give a list of rules to get you thinking about how to create a relationship and be part of one.

Love Rules...

1. Trust. If there is no trust, there is no relationship.

2. Give each other space. The main cause of relationships ending quickly is one partner making the other feel they are being suffocated. Nobody enjoys this!

3. Take time to get to know your new partner.

4. Compromise – it's no longer all about you.

5. Communicate your wants and listen to your partner's wants.

6. Appreciate their knowledge – true love flourishes from appreciation.

7. Always choose a partner who makes you laugh. A shared sense of humour is vital in a relationship.

8. Never undermine or humiliate your partner, especially in public.

9. Never mention the past unless asked; it allows comparison, which can damage self-esteem.

10. We all make mistakes and need to apologize when we do.

11. Nobody is perfect and no relationship is perfect. But in time you can implement changes that will help the relationship.

12. Always give your partner a second chance – you might need one yourself someday.

13. Be grateful for both small and large things.

14. Be extra nice to your partners' parents.

15. Take care of your looks and self-esteem. Your partner wants to be proud of you.

16. Passion comes first, but true love comes with time and sharing.

17. Sort out your priorities. Your partner will come first or second, depending on your baggage, as you will with them. Sometimes we need to be second for a while for a relationship to work, but one day, if it does work, we will be first.

18. Keep your friends and let your partner keep theirs.

19. If your partner is abusing themselves, make up your mind quickly whether or not you can handle it. The longer you leave it, the worse it will get. Offer a helping hand if they value you and want to get out of the abusive cycle.

20. Never swear at your partner or say hurtful words to them. The energy of an environment can be imprinted with negativity if this happens often.

21. Don't try to live your partner's life and don't let them live yours.

22. Be affectionate, hold hands, kiss out of the blue – life is short, so enjoy being in love.

CHAPTER 11

CREATIVITY AND CHILDREN

- *Element:* Metal

- *Direction:* Northern hemisphere: west; southern hemisphere: west

- *Animal:* Northern hemisphere: rooster; southern hemisphere: tiger

- *Parts of the Body:* Mouth, teeth, throat, larynx, kidneys, sexual organs, ears

- *Members of the Family:* Second son outside the home; third daughter inside the home

- *Imbalance:* An excess of fire items in this area causes an imbalance, as the fire melts the metal.

- *Solution:* Use metal as the main solution and earth as the second solution to activate the energy in this area.

I love the west – whether you are in the northern or southern hemisphere, it is the part of your property that relates to your imagination, your creativity, your higher self.

To work at its absolute best, the west must be calibrated with the east, working in balance with no obstacle lying between them. When you do your decluttering, make sure you clear all the junk from the west of your home or office, because that will immediately free up your creative energies.

The west also relates to children, so if you're having trouble getting pregnant you need to focus on this area, especially as the bedroom is often located here, because it's where the sun sets, so it helps people to gently shut down before bed.

Whenever I'm called to a home facing either east or west, I know it carries a lot of money in the middle of the property. The three elements relating to money are water, metal and earth, so when people call me because of money problems I check the middle of their home and very often they have a bathroom there, so all the money is disappearing down their toilet, basin or bath. We need to introduce more wood energy to balance out the water and stop the money from disappearing.

What if your property has the west missing? If it's missing on the inside, you will struggle to have children. If it's missing on the outside, it will affect your second child, particularly if it's a son, because there's male energy in this direction. Also related to it are the kidneys, ears and sexual organs, so you may have problems with these parts of the body.

Moving inside again, if that is missing, you will have a problem with your mouth or skin, which commonly manifests as eczema. This is often the result of a clash of elements, because the west's element is metal, which can easily clash with wood.

If you feel the need for more creativity in your life, look to the west. Make sure that it's clear of clutter and not full of heavy furniture. If it is, the moment you remove that weight, your creative juices will begin flowing. New energy, new ideas, new projects – you will be amazed. Adding a small fountain here will really help also, because the more the water flows, the more your creativity and money will flow, too.

One thing to remember if you are a creative person: it's very important to keep your ego in check, otherwise it will imbalance you and threaten your success. That's why so many people become famous for a very short period: their egos get out of control. We all want to feel confident and appreciated, but always remember who you are. You have to keep your feet on the ground and balance Heaven energy with Earth energy to achieve truly long-lasting success.

Let me give you an example of the importance of the west in fostering creativity. I was once asked to work with a graphic designer who was a very likeable, interesting guy. He lived with his girlfriend and was working in a room downstairs, but things weren't going well and he felt his creativity was blocked – his energy wasn't flowing and the business was struggling.

He wanted to be close to everyone downstairs, but the room he was working in was a little box room, whereas upstairs he had a huge loft with skylights, so there was plenty of natural light for him to work by, and you could even see the sunset from it. Plus, the ground floor represents the present, while the floors above represent the future, and the connection to Heaven was much stronger at the top of the house. So I said, 'Why don't you work here?'

That loft had lovely high ceilings. We painted the whole room white and the designer built a desk that ran from one wall to the other, so he had so much more room to work.

The other problem he had was that his girlfriend said he was always absent, always working, even when he was with her. Because it was his own business he was always trying to find new clients, either on the phone or the internet, so he was never truly relaxing or spending time with his girlfriend. This is a classic problem for creative types like designers, artists or writers: they're always thinking, always working. I always help them to separate work and rest and have a cut-off time every day when they stop. If not, they burn out, because we all need to rest and recuperate sometimes.

Once we moved the designer into the loft, he was able to isolate himself from everyone else and just focus on work. When he came down, he closed the door and work was done for the day, so he could completely focus on his partner.

After making the changes, he commented that he was feeling inspired to create. That was due to the fact that he was closer to Heaven and the change of position had got the energy working. Also, on the ground floor he had no views from the windows, but on the top floor he did, so the future was totally unblocked and he felt better about it.

It was important to connect him with the west visually, spiritually and energetically, and in the loft he had that connection – he gazed out in that direction all day and could watch beautiful sunsets through those huge windows. Creative professionals must always look to open space, and having a view of the sky is perfect. Creativity comes from Heaven energy and it is important to be in touch with it.

This designer's creativity started flowing again and his business became so successful that he was able to rent an office. It's a very nice story and I'm so glad I could help him achieve the success he deserved.

If you work from home, make sure your work space is airy and light and above all you are comfortable. If you are starting your own business, the west can be a useful area. If it is well decorated and you feel good about it, you will be able to improve your product through constant inspiration. In many of the businesses with financial and product issues I have visited, the west was missing.

When you run your own business, you must make sure you communicate well, and this direction is related to the mouth, therefore balancing it improves communication, too.

Balancing the west will really help you with the opposite direction, too, which relates to the family, and you will notice that communication will improve here as well. By unblocking the west of the home you may clear any issues you may have with your partner or parents.

The west benefits from the earth element, because it supports the metal energy in this direction, so painting the walls a very pale jasmine or yellowy off-white is perfect. Just make sure it's very, very pale. This way, whichever hemisphere you are in, you will be able to get great benefits from this direction.

The west is also famous for fertility – particularly for women getting pregnant with their first child. If you are trying to have a baby, make sure that there are no heavy items of furniture in the west or any obstacles on your path.

Whatever you are trying to create, as I said earlier, the most important thing you can do is to declutter. And, like all the best feng shui cures, that doesn't cost a thing.

This is a lovely exercise to do once you have decluttered the west and painted the walls so the area is light, beautiful and inspiring:

1. Invite three people working in the same field as you to your house. After some refreshments, get everyone to sit in a circle or around a circular table with a candle in the middle and sit quietly for 10 minutes. You could all do a breathing exercise or creative visualization – whatever you are all comfortable with.

2. When you are all relaxed and calm, decide who is A, B, C and D. A should work with B and C with D. A begins by telling B everything they think and feel about their creativity, what's blocking them and where they should go in the future. Then B does the same to C, C to D and D to A. It's a good idea for the person listening to make notes about what they are receiving.

3. Then discuss your notes. What was accurate? What felt right to you? What was useful? The amazing thing about this exercise is that even if your partner knows nothing about you, you'll find that 30–50 per cent of what they tell you is really accurate.

4. What you do with that feedback is up to you, but most people find it really helps clarify where they are, where they want to be in future and how to get there.

People always love this exercise, so you should definitely try it. It can be very interesting to learn how you are perceived by other professionals. Creative people in particular tend to work by themselves and can be isolated, but it is really important that they communicate their skills and ideas.

CHAPTER 12

FRIENDS, MENTORS AND NETWORKING

- *Element:* Metal

- *Direction:* Northern hemisphere: northwest; southern hemisphere: southwest

- *Animal:* Northern hemisphere: dog and pig; southern hemisphere: rat and ox

- *Parts of the Body:* Head, lungs, colon, brain, mind, arms, hands

- *Members of the Family:* Third son outside the home; father inside the home

- *Imbalance:* An excess of fire items in this area causes an imbalance, as the fire melts the metal.

- *Solution:* Use metal as the main solution and earth as the second solution to activate the energy in this area.

Although this area is mainly about our friends, it also holds a very strong spiritual energy. Because of this, it's the place to put an altar or symbol of whatever religion means most to you.

On a more practical level, if you're looking for help from others, perhaps someone to help you with your office or your home, this is the direction you must focus on. This way you will have the benefit of having people coming to you with good advice. When this direction is energized, mentors will come to you and you will be able to network successfully. A great deal of prosperity can come through networking both in your work and friendship environment, so be prepared to accept the help of others. If you don't have a window here, however, you will have trouble finding help, because you won't be able to receive Heaven energy.

There is also a powerful male energy in this direction, so problems here will affect the man of the house. If a woman is looking for a partner, it's very important she checks the interior of her home and makes sure this direction is present. I have tried many cures for a missing friends area and have managed to bring a lot of masculine energy to homes without it, but nothing has ever been as effective as a property that had it in the first place. It's a tricky one.

I once did some research on these types of properties. In an apartment block where this direction was missing, 60 per cent of the women were either single or widowed. That shows you how important this direction is, especially for straight women!

I remember a client in Italy who had moved into a new flat with her boyfriend. The northwest was missing completely, and it really affected their relationship. The boyfriend was absent more and more, travelling all the time. Eventually, he left my client for someone he met on his travels and she found it really hard to meet anyone else. At the same time, the market dropped so she couldn't sell her property. That was also partly due to the missing northwest, because it's directly opposite the southeast, which is the direction relating to money in the northern hemisphere. Despite the feng shui advice, this client stayed in the flat. She is still single.

I always recommend charity work to people having problems generating what they want in life. The more they help others, the more help they will receive in return. As I said earlier, it's also ideal to have a window in the friends area, so install one if you can. Keep the area very tidy, too, and introduce the metal element, possibly by painting the walls white. A little fire energy is also good and even earth, so pale yellow or other off-white colours are also perfect for northwestern walls.

One thing I would say is that if you have a clash of elements in this direction, it will directly affect the man. So, if the man of the house is having health problems, check out this direction. There may well be too much wood clashing with metal, or an excess of water in the property's interior. It's important to ask a feng shui consultant to help you improve the layout, colour scheme and elements.

The more masculine this direction becomes, the better, so try hanging pictures of men or heroic male figures on the walls. Or, if you have a front door in this direction, paint it a metallic colour, like white or silver, or add a metal doorknob. This will also help balance your finances.

One thing about properties missing this direction is they tend to be very good properties for gay couples because they carry both yin and yang energies. In feng shui we say that gay people have mixed *chi* energy – a little of both qualities.

This direction is also to do with friendships. It is always good if our dinner table is here, as it will energize parties and entertaining.

With friendship you must focus on quality rather than quantity. Give and take and balance must be present; if a friend makes it all about them most of the time, ask yourself whether there is any true concern there for you. Good friends are like family and you will keep them for ever, because unconditional love will take over and you will always be there for one another. Most friendships don't start out this way, of course, but the energy changes over time as you realize how much you care for these friends.

If you are dealing with friends who are addicted to drugs, or indeed if you are yourself, it is important to change the energy in the friends direction so that you won't be constantly reminded of your past and slip back into the same patterns. Addiction can be genetically programmed, but also can be a choice. Willpower must take over and that is why it is important to have a small altar here to introduce more Heaven energy into your life. When whatever you are addicted to has power over you it means your soul isn't inside your body and you don't feel you are present in the here and now. To correct that you must connect to the pure light of Heaven. You can do this through prayer, through spiritual healing or simply by asking your loved ones on the other side to help you. If you are trying or know someone who is trying to beat addiction I really recommend spiritual healing. In no time your soul will be back and your willpower will take over and guide you to a positive result.

One final word: having friends means you will never be alone, but if after a while you feel certain friendships aren't going to move into unconditional friendship, let them go, because it isn't healthy to confide in someone who isn't really there for you. Luck in friendship and health go well together.

This exercise is about taking stock of your friends and relationships in general:

1. Start by sitting quietly and taking stock to see how much you give to the world around you. Are your friendships conditional? Do you give only to receive? If so, you need to make some changes.

2. Think hard about your friends and the way you interact with them. Remember that it's far better to have a few friends with whom you are truly intimate than 100 acquaintances who hardly know you. When you give of your time, love or energy to these true

friends, do so without any expectation. That way you will receive many good things in return – usually far more than you have given.

3. If, on the other hand, you have friends with vampire abilities – taking all your energy and never giving anything back to replace it – I recommend you clear them. What you can do is imagine a light around yourself and a light around the person that needs to go and see a pair of scissors gently cut the connection between you around the stomach area. Send them healing as you do so and ask them to move on to something that is better for them. This way you will be setting yourself free, but from the moment you cut the cord, expect an immediate bounce effect: those very same people will call you because you are no longer feeding the friendship and the vampire will get hungry. You must resist, because by saving that energy you will start feeling better about yourself and strong about the choice you made.

Sometimes we have a really hard time letting go of friendships that aren't good for us. There can be resistance to overcome, but if we persevere, the transformation will occur.

What you feed will grow – you are the person with the power. Help yourself and universe will help you.

CHAPTER 13

FENG SHUI GUIDELINES

Now we have looked at each of the directions, here are some general feng shui guidelines to help you on your way to creating luck.

To begin with, dream about how you want your life to be. Luck is all about believing that good things are possible and you can make them happen.

In order to do so, though, you do need to take responsibility for all that has happened in your life. Dealing with the feelings from your past will allow you to face the future with honesty and to think positively even when times are tough. So try to let go of any bad experiences, sadness or resentment and do whatever you need to do to leave them in the past. This will instigate change for the better and a few alterations to your home can accelerate the process.

First Impressions

Look around your home and see if there is anything that disturbs your comfort and acts as an obstacle to change. Remember that it's incredibly important to be happy with your home. When you stand outside your front door, what do you see? Is your house balanced? Are both sides of your home in equilibrium?

Remember the importance of balancing the three energies. When purchasing a penthouse, for example, be aware that it has a lot of Heaven energy, so make sure you balance it out with Earth energy. I find that elderly people living on top of buildings end up getting sick very easily because the energy is too strong for them if the property isn't balanced properly.

What do you feel as you look at your property? Does it attract you? An issue I have often encountered is that a property can be very well decorated but have no life. Although such properties look good, no one uses them because the energy isn't seductive. Usually this is because the number of occupants is out of proportion with the size of the property.

Use your feelings, good or bad, as a guide to the changes you might make to your property. The ideas in this book will help you.

The Entrance

Starting with the entrance, make sure it's illuminated and that the main door is clean and tidy. It is the mouth of the house, so any decay or breakages must be repaired immediately.

The size of your front door is very important, because *chi* flows from the street through the front door and it's vital to grab it. Make sure the front door is in proportion to the house. It is also important to have a larger front door and smaller back door, as the back door is where you take your rubbish out. In properties without a back door, some feng shui consultants treat the toilet as a back door.

If you have a front door facing the back door, this can be a problem, as the energy will flow too fast and you might have a hard time holding on to it. This will cause other rooms in the property to stagnate, which can have financial implications.

It is important to think about what impact a property has on you as you walk through the front door. If you see the kitchen first, you will always be reminded about food, which may result in obesity, especially in years when your horoscope isn't particularly auspicious.

The Kitchen

A good kitchen should be either square or rectangular. In the northern hemisphere the northeast is a good place for it and in the southern hemisphere the southwest.

In the kitchen it is very important not to place elements that clash opposite each other. For example, the stove (fire) should not face the sink (water). My studies have shown that this clash creates arguments in the house. It's better to place a sink and stove next to each other.

The Hall

Hallways should be clear of obstacles, because they work like the arteries in our bodies. Energy should be able to flow around a house.

I find that clients who like to hold on to their possessions, piling them up in rooms, hallways and every possible corner, have a lot of health issues resulting from confusion in the mind. A good general rule is to clear all the clutter in your home and let everything go easily.

The Bedroom

A bedroom is a place for sleeping, so the emptier it is, the better.

As for the bed, as a basic guideline, if you are an early-rising person place your bedroom in the northeast or east in the northern hemisphere and east and southeast in the southern hemisphere. If you are a late riser, place it in the northwest or west in the northern hemisphere and southwest or west in the southern hemisphere.

Make sure your bed has a headboard or solid wall behind it for support and your bedroom is painted a very pale colour, so you can relax when you go to bed. Don't place your bed between two doors, for example an en-suite bathroom door and a bedroom door.

Having your bed under a beam can cut the *chi* energy and make you uncomfortable in bed. This effect is so strong I have seen couples divorce due to the pressure on the marriage. Beams can also lead to headaches and pains in the body.

Another problem in the bedroom can be a wall pointing at the bed. We call this *sha chi*, or poison arrows. They can cause health issues and even lead to a couple separating. The solution for both beams and poison arrows is simply shaping the edges of the beam or wall to make them more rounded.

Too many electronic devices by your bed can disturb sleep. Also, the body does carry a small amount of electricity and that can connect with the equipment. To be safe, any electrical equipment needs to be six feet away from the bed. Outside the house, be aware of any electricity pylons or mobile phone masts. Research has demonstrated that they can affect the health of the occupants.

One of the most famous rules of feng shui is not to have a mirror opposite the bed. This is because if you wake up during the night and are frightened by your reflection in the mirror, it will make you oversensitive and afraid during the day. It is like disturbing your soul.

If you want a relationship, make sure your bedroom is designed for two people, so it's ready for your future partner.

If you live in an apartment, it is important to buy a bed that lets air flow underneath. This will help you sleep better and not draw the energy or noise from the flat below.

The Toilet

When designing a home, try not to place the toilet opposite the front door, because this will cause a loss of energy and the occupants of the house will feel drained. In general, we need to be careful where we place toilets. Feng shui consultants normally use the house's astrology to determine the best position. It's good for toilets to have a window and to be painted white, to express clean and light energy.

Make sure you don't have a toilet in the middle of your home. That is an area that is the heart of the home and should not be disturbed.

Toilets are good in your unlucky personal directions: *Liu Sha*, *Wu Kwei*, *Chueg Ming* and *Huo Hai*.

In the general directions chart (see page 54), make sure you don't have a toilet in the wealth direction – for obvious reasons.

Outside the Property

Take account of what you are looking at outside your windows. I have visited many businesses that are renting premises because they are cheap, but in the long run this is harming the business because the outlook is poor and that will reflect back on the business.

The shape of the road outside a property and the way the traffic flows will have an influence on it. If you face a

T-junction that can seriously affect your business or home, as the energy will flow to your front door too strongly.

Trees directly in front of your door may be harmful, but if they are in the friends direction they may bring you a position of authority among your friends.

A long time ago I visited a PR consultant who was finding it difficult to find new clients. When I looked out of her office window, there was another building blocking the view, so there was no future for the company. I advised her to make some small changes in the short term, but to move offices in the long run. She has done so now and the number of her clients has doubled.

Moving On...

Many people get used to the direction of the home they are living in, so be aware that if you are looking for a property, one might feel right just because it faces the same way as your present home. This can be misleading, because a change might be better for you. 'If you keep doing what you've always done, you'll get what you've always got', as they say, and it's certainly true of property. If you keep moving to properties that face the same way, you'll always get the same results in terms of your personal luck.

Your home is a sacred place and if you can't love it and want to move on, do something that will make the energy better: give it light, talk to the walls if necessary and call upon your ancestors to help you to sort the problem out. But at the same time, send your thoughts out to the home you want to create. That way you will program your subconscious to make it happen. When you truly believe that you deserve good things, it becomes much easier to be positive, and slowly but surely you will enjoy a change in fortune.

N

NE

PART II

HUMAN ENERGY

W

E

SW

SE

S

*'What the mind of man can conceive
and believe, it can achieve.'*
NAPOLEON HILL

CHAPTER 14

LOOK WITHIN

Take a moment to ask yourself what you are feeling now. Are you free? Are you doing what you want to do? Are you afraid of not having enough? Do you believe that you aren't going to be able to survive by doing what you want to do? Do you find it easy to be secure, happy or optimistic? Or is it easier to be judgemental or critical of others and yourself?

Our exterior world is a reflection of our interior world, so stop now and consider what you are bringing into your life.

Fear

We might say we only want to bring the best into our life. But so often we encounter resistance to the changes that we would like to make – resistance that comes from within. As humans, we are afraid of change.

Psychologically, it is proven that people are happier when they are secure. The moment we have the courage to experiment with freedom, uncertainty arrives, and it can be a shock when the life we were avoiding is on our doorstep. The choice can be overwhelming. Shall I do this or shall I do that?

To be sure we are on the right path, we need to follow our head *and* our heart. Sometimes we are overwhelmed with physical tiredness and those moments are not good for making decisions. A good night's sleep can sometimes make challenges seem completely different.

When we go to sleep at night, we absorb spiritually all the knowledge we have accumulated during the day and our brain will either discharge it through dreams or keep it in our subconscious. We can also leave our body and go astral travelling – the number of people who have told me about these experiences is amazing. Sometimes the spirit world will take us into the future, so that our soul can be at peace. Then, when we wake up the next day, we will experience a feeling of reassurance about the decisions we are facing. So, if you don't know what to do, go to bed!

At the moment, evolution is taking place too quickly and is making the pace of life very fast. We are all hurtling along too fast to stop and enjoy the moment. That pace is already making people leave the big cities in search of more peace. Moving away may seem the most appropriate thing to do, but we will only find peace if it is inside us.

From time to time we all become victims of our social environment at home or at work and are controlled by fear. This is only natural and we shouldn't waste time criticizing ourselves for it, but simply focus on the positive. Then energy will follow intention and luck will follow that. This is the best use of our Human energy.

So, change your thoughts of fear to feelings of safety. Then a spiritual power will take over and manifest safety in your life.

No matter what is happening around you, if you keep calm and maintain silence within, from that silence you will get the answers you need.

Fear itself is not a good adviser. It isn't realistic to expect it to be absent entirely, but remember that you must face it and look at where it is coming from. It may well have a parenting background. This again shows the importance of coming to terms with your past and establishing a good relationship with your parents. You will find that once you have dealt with that, you can understand and deal with many of your fears.

It is interesting that just as you prepare to change, you will often sabotage yourself in some way, especially by means of procrastination, or maybe by getting a cold or becoming lethargic. This, too, can be a manifestation of fear.

You have to have persistence to overcome fear, but it will be worth it – persistence will keep you focused on the prize and then fear will fade away, because it is all in your mind. The world will become your oyster and you will create luck.

Fear can also lead to greed, which is a great enemy. It is usually based on the fear of not having enough. I truly believe that when we are greedy it is the result of suffering grave hardship in the past and never trusting life again. This insecurity lives on in our mind, but it is just a thought. Thoughts, however, can have quite an impact.

The Power of Thought

Our thoughts can make or break us. Their power was shown as far back as the early twentieth century, when Napoleon Hill's persistence in studying the effects of thought proved that if you think something, you can make it happen.

What are thoughts? They are the process of creation in our minds, and this process will realize our deepest desires. How does that happen? In my view our thoughts have a 'bounce effect' on our psyche and what many people regard as coincidence is the result of a deeper contact with our own soul through the power of thought.

Focused thought has the power of manifestation, both good and bad. It is also true that there is a link between daydreaming and thinking. When we are wishing unconsciously in this way it activates our loved ones in the spirit world to help us on Earth.

Thoughts carry power, so be careful not to exercise your will over others. Set them free and think only about your own luck, but do pray for others to find their own way in the school of life.

The value of thought is immense because it creates our beliefs. As an example, if two people are trying to lose weight and follow exactly the same diet but one believes it will work and the other doesn't, the believer will lose weight and the other won't. It can be as simple as that.

My mum always tells me whatever you believe will work. We are the gasoline for our thoughts, and in the silence within us, we can breed peace or harm.

The motivation for everything comes from thought – and that includes fear. If you empower fear, it will turn into reality. In this respect, it is important to be aware of the news you read and what you allow yourself to believe. Don't pollute your brain with the shock of negative news and be tempted to let fear grow. The solutions to your challenges will come if you focus on *positive* thought.

Willpower

Creating luck is a lot about willpower. When this is strong, our intentions are focused and our plans are therefore likely to come to fruition.

This all starts with respecting ourselves and what we want rather than comparing ourselves to those around us. Comparison happens in all cultures, but this is tribal behaviour. The key to creating luck isn't competition, it's creation. It is all about *you* – what you focus on and whether you think you deserve to succeed.

The journey to success isn't always straightforward, but it's important not to lose focus and give up along the way. I would like to tell you the story of how I learned never to lose hope. (You will also find this story in a book called *Por mi, por mi casa y por lo que me esperas* by Terry Guindi.)

Many years ago I was invited by an amazing client, Terry Guindi, to Mexico for some feng shui work, including a weekend of fun in Acapulco. The afternoon before we left we stopped at a shop that sold crystals to purchase some articles to be used in the feng shui consultation. When we got back into the car Terry gave me a crystal ball she had purchased in the form of an amethyst. She had seen me holding it, felt I liked it and decided to give it to me as a present to bind our friendship.

I was thrilled with the present. I couldn't let go of it on the flight I loved it so much!

It was sunny in Acapulco and the next day Terry and her son Alberto lounged by the pool while I met a friend who needed counselling and we worked for an hour together.

Once my meeting was over, I decided to go to the beach and take my new crystal ball with me so that I could cleanse it in the sea. Seawater has healing powers and sea air makes us healthy and happy, due to the negative ions it contains.

As I was walking by the sea holding the amethyst, I felt happiness taking over my soul and energizing the beautiful stone. In my mind I was asking the universe to empower the crystal to raise my spirit every time I felt down. I was also empowering it with love from my own energy and connection to Heaven. I loved it and was grateful for its presence in my life.

With my back to the sea, I raised the amethyst to the sun – and was suddenly knocked over by a massive wave. I didn't know it at the time, but the currents in Acapulco are the strongest in Mexico and have killed many people.

I went rolling and as I stood up I realized my stone had disappeared. I was horrified, but then I heard was a voice saying, 'Seek and you shall find.' It was a moment of magic and I became very calm.

I saw Terry running towards me, desperate to see if I was alright. I told her to mark the spot where I was standing while I went to change into some shorts so I could look for the stone closer to the sea. She immediately offered to buy me another one, but I said, 'You don't need to do that – I placed love in this one and we will find it. And when we do, I will let you name it.'

Terri waited patiently on the spot until I got back. She was really afraid that I was going to be swept away again, so she stayed glued to me and didn't allow me to go in the sea at all. We started looking for the stone and then Alberto arrived, so there were three of us looking.

As time passed, hope started fading. After half an hour my friends wanted me to stop looking, as they felt that the stone would have sunk in the sand and would be impossible to find.

My heart was sinking too, but I remembered a Winston Churchill saying, 'Never, never, never give up,' and I thought, 'Come on, universe, give me my crystal back. It is well cleansed and will be with me for the rest of my life and I want it now!'

Positive focus like this will combine with your spiritual power and create a reaction – in this case it was like a miracle, but the only divine intervention was that of my mind.

'It's here!' Terry shouted. 'I've found it! I've found it!'

She was about 50 yards away from where I had lost the crystal and had been walking in the sand when she had felt the stone buried under her foot.

As we dug out the stone, Terry named it Hester. We baptized it in the sea. All three of us were so happy, and what's more, I'd been taught never to lose hope. That lesson was not just for me but for all of us. The power of the place, the power of the energy and our own power had all combined with the power of Heaven to make the impossible happen.

The stone is always in sight as I write. It reminds me that everything is possible and our intentions have the power to transform our world.

Little did I know the day before, when I walked into the shop, that an amethyst would change my life in a profound way. There is a reason for every event in our lives. So watch what is going on around you and listen to the messages, because you are in constant communication with the soul inside you and that soul will show you your true path. Just keep calm and then you can listen to the guidance that will come to you.

Heart and Hormones

Our emotions and willpower go together and are part of the physical and hormonal movement in our body. We behave according to how we feel inside – nature has its cycles and hormonal movement plays a large role in these.

As adolescents, for example, when we get out and about and want to find love and reproduce, we smell one another's necks and let the pheromones take over.

When we mature, we will maybe get married, have kids and work hard, going through many emotions and relying on willpower as we do so, then halfway through our lives the hormonal pace will slow down and at around 30 to 40 years old we will settle down, maybe gain weight and hopefully find contentment.

After that, nature will give us our youth hormones back for at least another three years, and that is where the danger lies. At that point we will have realized that life isn't for ever and will probably have started questioning what we have done with it so far – it's a recipe for a midlife crisis!

Our emotions will be really mixed up at this time and it is important to do a reality check. It is also critical to seek support from our partners. We must not spoil a perfect relationship, especially if it involves kids, just because we are going through hormonal change. We need to keep the channels of communication open with our partner or friends to let all our emotions out. Rather than jumping into something new or being impulsive, we should share our feelings.

Some of the clients I have met have got divorced at this age, only to find out two years later that they made a mistake. Some have remarried, but others have never got back what they had before.

On a positive note, this is the time when women start expressing themselves and realizing their dreams. As their kids leave home, they have the opportunity to do what they always wanted. Hillary Clinton is an example of this – she gained power and recognition later in life and started pursuing her true passion after she was 45 years old.

Oprah Winfrey's television programmes are sometimes dedicated to people who made things happen later in life. Maybe the saying that life starts at 40 is true after all. Think about it – maybe that is the time when we really learn to love life and realize we can make a difference in the world.

The Power of Love

One thing that is part of our whole life, from birth to passing, is giving and receiving love. If you think about it, life itself is all about love and anything else is worthless – there is no point achieving the highest honours, having the healthiest bank account, owning many properties and having the most amazing career if you have no love in your life. Even true health is only possible if we love ourselves. We can also be healed though love or heal others through giving it.

When you base your life on giving and receiving unconditional love you don't need much to be happy. And yet, paradoxically, unconditional love leads to generosity, which in turn will trigger abundance.

If you have never been shown how to love others or yourself, I hope that this book will help you to learn. If you are looking for material things to cover your lack of love, it's time to wake up.

It's never too late to learn how to love. It starts with a thought – a loving thought. You might start by giving time to an elderly person or choosing a cause and doing something to support it. Myself, I like to have a finger in many pies, but mostly I make time for children and the elderly. My personal friends also have a particular space in my heart and I hug and kiss them whenever I get the chance. It's always valuable to share our truth with friends and feel that we matter to them.

If you find it hard expressing love with humans, I advise you to adopt an animal. They are usually quick to offer unconditional love and they do not charge.

Why not do something nice every day for someone? The universe does give us opportunities, so take them. Appreciate every moment and be grateful for the opportunities to help someone along the way. This way you will activate abundance in all areas.

Don't forget to express love for yourself, too. You might be surprised by the impact this can have on your life. People who don't love themselves are often very busy – they make sure they are occupied every minute of the day to compensate for the emptiness they feel within. They usually talk about many things, too, but they just can't talk about themselves. The truth is that they would prefer to live someone else's life than their own. Self-empowerment is not in their vocabulary. Courage may be there, but stifled by their past or by pure laziness. So life is stressful and the person just accepts that and feels they don't deserve any better. But we all deserve the best out of life and we can create it.

Loving ourselves starts with compassion. We must have compassion for ourselves and others, along with the courage to forgive ourselves and others and above all to commit to true healing. This could include asking others to forgive us, too. That is how love starts flowing in our heart.

We will be creating a lot of luck this way, because to be truly successful we need the goodwill of others. When we lose this because we aren't nice to people, we create an aura around us that can make things go really wrong for us.

To change this vibration, we need to have respect for ourselves and respect for others as fellow humans. A simple way to start is just to stop for a moment and talk to anyone who gives you attention. You will soon see how others open up to you. Why not shock people by saying hello to them in the street? Look them in the eyes and see their soul and you will be using your Heaven and Human energies together.

When we make changes in our lives it is also important to have respect for both others and ourselves. If we can make changes without being controlling or breaking boundaries, we will become successful because our spirit will radiate an abundance of love.

The only lesson we came to Earth for is the lesson of love. So open your mind, open your heart and above all open your eyes and let love flow in and out of you. Give it and receive it at every opportunity. Life is based on love and all you will take with you is love when you pass, so forget everything else and start focusing on love. Then you will find luck coming your way, too.

Live in the Moment

It is part of life to enjoy the moment. Don't worry about accumulating riches – just aim to be comfortable and enjoy life. I don't see the point of having a big house to prove something and not being able to go out.

I have an infinite number of stories of people who worked throughout their lives to create security in retirement, only to retire at 60 and die at 65. What's the point of that? It is far better to enjoy what we do so that it becomes pleasurable and no longer feels like a job.

Even when you do retire, you can still enjoy what you do. I have heard over and over that the formula for longevity is to have a busy mind and to keep working in whatever field you choose at least once a week. If you have to retire from your profession, you can still volunteer for a charity, dedicate your life to doing good, fight for a cause, have dignity and respect for yourself and enjoy life in perhaps unexpected ways. And you can open yourself up spiritually and create luck along the way!

I must express my admiration for 'retired' people who are helping other beings to grow. Their souls are working not for money but out of unconditional love. Remember we won't take any material possessions with us when we pass to the spirit world, just the unconditional love we planted.

So, don't worry, be happy. Humans are natural worriers. It doesn't take much and off we go, let's worry! But that doesn't get us anywhere.

Worry can be easily dealt with by trusting life, or, better, our soul. I always say we mustn't worry about how to live life, just live it to the full at every moment.

Life goes by very quickly, so enjoy it right now – don't waste time accumulating or competing to have things when you could be spreading your love and being loved.

Then, once you are happy with your environment and have a balanced Human life, the next step is to make your connection to Heaven.

N

NE

PART III
HEAVEN ENERGY

W

E

SW

SE

S

'You don't have a soul. You are a soul.
You have a body.'
C. S. LEWIS

CHAPTER 15

CONNECTIONS

Heaven energy is often left out of the equation when people are seeking a change of fortune, but it is the energy that makes everything happen and connecting to it is sure to create luck.

A client who works in a bank rang me some time ago. Due to the financial crisis, he was worried about his job. I told him to connect to his soul. He asked me how. I told him to pray and trust he would get an answer.

Almost 12 months went by and I heard from him again. He told me he had done what I recommended and prayed hard. His job was to create formulas for banks and he told me that a week later he had been inspired to try a different formula, which had resulted in profits for his bank. He had been promoted to manager of his department and was now up for a bonus.

That banker prayed for guidance, but how we make our connection to Heaven energy is up to us. The main thing to remember is that we must manage our own life and make sure our tribe isn't doing it for us. So, whether we follow a traditional religious path or not, we should make sure it is our own choice.

In feng shui, Heaven energy enters the equation through the astrology of a building and its occupants. Certain buildings are also able to carry the energy of people who died in them or people who loved them, and many mediums are able to detect it. Belief in life after death is paramount here. Many people nowadays have lost this belief, but nevertheless the spirit world is always with us.

When I was a child I had 'imaginary' friends like any other child, but I could see mine until I was five years old and went to school. Looking back, I was a lonely child and quite isolated, so it made sense that spirits played with me. That is how I discovered we are never alone.

At 13 years old I had a dream. Going through puberty was horrible and I was depressed because I knew I was different. But in the dream I saw a light and felt uplifted by unconditional love. In the light part of my future was shown to me and I saw that I would live in another country. When I woke up, everything was better. My soul had always known where we were going and now that I knew, too, I felt healed and happy as I was.

After that, connections were made that led me to go to the UK to study and eventually make the country my permanent home. I was meant to be there.

I was also meant to develop as a healer and a medium, though I didn't realize it for a while. It was a very interesting time in my life. I was dumped by my first love, lost my job, fell ill and couldn't see the way forward. In bed most of the time, I depended on acquaintances who have now become my lifelong friends.

I noted during that time that my ability to hear and see spirits was stronger. It sounds crazy, but one of my great uncles, who had passed away five years earlier, used to come by every day at the same time to check up on me. I was physically alone, but spiritually enlightened by his presence. One day he told me he was not dead. His earthly body was, because there is a life span, a sell-by date, for everything in the material world, but his spirit lived on. We all do, and there will be a big party when we get to the other side.

Each one of us is part of a group of souls who come to Earth together to undertake the spiritual learning that we need. So every moment of our lives is driven by spirituality. It is like a game, and we will always be challenged along the way. We might think we can win, but actually there are no winners, just achievers of enlightenment.

On the other side, souls can be at many places at the same time and we can call upon them if we wish. So our loved ones who have gone to the spirit world have never really left us. In bad times they will always be there to help us. Spirits will often manifest in this world, either to bring messages or, if people are grieving, to reassure them that they are OK. So mediumship is a wonderful way to help the bereaved. It uplifts those left on Earth and gives proof that our loved ones are still around as souls.

We often suffer a lot because we value our bodies so much. It is good to take care of your body, but it is ultimately just a vessel for your soul and it has an expiry date. This will be determined by genetics and not because you had negative thoughts, by the way, so chill!

As for what happened to me, eventually I met a friend by chance on the tube and she took the time to guide me to a Spiritualist church where my healing path as a patient and as a healer started. It was all because that friend really cared. Her name was Maria Cunha and if there are angels on this Earth, she is one of them. We have been friends for 27 years and she enabled me to develop my connection to the spirit world. I found classes were available through the College of Psychic Studies in London, was reassured that there were other people out there seeing and hearing spirits, and realized I was free to be a medium. That was it – I never looked back. In my heart I knew I was where I had to be.

During my years at the college I learned that development comes gradually. The spirit world prepares us and it is only after we have had enough life experiences that spirits come through so that we can help others. We need a certain level of maturity first.

Eventually I ended up doing platform work in Spiritualist churches, passing messages to the public. To this day I like to support the Spiritualist movement and I go and see mediums at Spiritualist churches. I still do platform work, but only for the church or charitable causes. I see mediumship as a gift that is there to help others and not for entertainment.

One day, at a service at Woodford Spiritualist church, I passed a message to a friend called Reggie. He was himself an active medium and supported me in my platform work every time I went to Woodford.

Reggie had been invited to become a minister but was questioning the request because he was already in his eighties. However, his mother in the spirit world was asking me to tell him that he should take it on. He said the invitation hadn't come from a Spiritualist church and that was another reason why he wasn't sure, but immediately his mother said that it didn't matter. 'Spirit will still work through you,' she said, 'because spirit has many clothes.'

The spirit world has plans for us all, so relax, be flexible and enjoy what comes your way. Create something with it. When you connect with your soul, you will create luck, so set yourself free of any limiting beliefs and let your spirit flow. Talk to yourself and you will get answers very quickly. Don't be afraid to talk out loud! You aren't crazy, you are powerful and getting in touch with your soul!

Mediumship takes time to develop, as I mentioned earlier, but can provide amazing proof of life after death. Many people really have a hard time with this, due to tribal beliefs, and they say to leave the dead alone, but in reality what dies is only our physical part. The soul lives on, and if a soul wishes to communicate with those left on Earth, why not?

Sooner or later the spirit world makes itself known to all of us, even if it is on our deathbed! Many people see their departed loved ones just before their own passing, as they come to reassure them that it OK to go with them and move on.

Also, as I mentioned earlier, I believe that our parents can guide us in life, whether they are in this world or the next. It is often easier for parents to communicate with their children from the spirit world than from this one!

Once we ourselves pass to the other side, our mission is first to rest, and that can take up to six months. I have received messages from people who died just weeks before, but that is only possible with the help of other souls. After six to twelve months our soul will gain strength and our post-graduate course in life will begin. Our mission then will be to watch over our loved ones to help them to learn their earthly lessons. These loved ones can include friends and soul mates who haven't incarnated in the form of family – unconditional love is the key here.

So, from our perspective on Earth, we can be reassured that no matter how bad things get, the spirit world can help us. I remember the story of a woman I met in Stockwell Spiritualist church one day. She told me that when she lost her husband, it was really hard to cope as she had a disabled child who needed an organ transplant. Life was becoming unbearable, so she decided to commit suicide.

She was going to jump in front of a train, so she drove to a particular station, went down to the platform and sat down, waiting for a fast train. When she realized the train was coming she stood up, but the thought of what she was about to do was too much for her and she fainted. People rushed to help her and as she woke up she heard a voice telling her to go to a church, so she left the station with someone's help, got back in her car and drove without a direction in mind.

At the first church she saw, she parked her car and walked in. It happened to be a Spiritualist church, a place she had never considered visiting. She stayed for a service and the medium gave her a message from her husband. He told her that he was well and loved her and was going to make everything alright for her. As she sat there in the church, she felt as if a weight had been lifted from her.

She left the church and went home, and as she walked through the front door she found her mother and child getting ready to go to hospital, because an organ donor had been found...

You must trust that life will never give you more than you can handle. Whatever your challenge, focus on the solution, because if something is in your life, you *can* handle it. Also, know that you are supported on your journey through life.

Synchronicity

Proof that we are being watched over can come in many ways, often through meaningful coincidences in a process known as synchronicity. This concept was first explored by the psychiatrist Carl Gustav Jung. I first came across his work whilst at Roehampton University, where I spent a year studying psychology and health. I found it a fascinating explanation of how mind and matter came together.

Now I believe that synchronicity is the workings of a group of spirits – some family members, others not – who are guiding us throughout our life. They will pass messages to us in many different forms – some through 'coincidences', some through the promptings of our intuition, some in mediumistic fashion. We all have the ability to sense these messages; in fact I believe we all become mediums at some stage in our lives. We can also connect with our guardian angels and they can send messages in many diverse ways.

Recently I was talking about the power of prayer to a client and she told me the story of a friend of hers who had been very ill and had had to give up her job and apply for benefits. There was just one issue: she couldn't find her passport and she needed it for her application. She turned her house upside down and was desperate.

My client told her, 'Don't worry, I will come to you with a candle a priest has given me and we will pray that you find your passport.'

They did this and that night her sick friend had a dream in which the priest and several angels were telling her not to worry and that things would be alright. In the dream she felt reassured and at peace.

The next day she woke up feeling really well and unusually calm. She decided to pray again and this time she also said the Apostles' creed and prayed to Archangel Michael. Afterwards she started looking for her passport again, but still couldn't find it. Lunchtime came and she hadn't found the passport so she went to cook a meal and just then the phone started ringing.

When she answered it, there was a gentleman on the other end who told her that he had been trying to contact her for almost 10 months. She explained to him that she had been in hospital all that time. Then he said that he was in possession of her passport, as she had left it behind in his office.

In shock, she told him, 'I can't leave my house, but I will get a friend to come and collect it.'

Immediately he told her not to worry, as he would deliver it.

When she opened the door to him, she felt light and warmth radiating from him. He simply smiled at her, said, 'Here it is,' and left.

She called my client and told her that when she had met the man she had felt the same feeling that she had had in the dream. She believed there was an angel inside him. It had been just 72 hours since she had started praying.

Heaven energy is closer than we think.

One morning quite a long time ago I realized my cat was behaving strangely. He wouldn't allow me to touch him and wouldn't eat his food. As he was purring, I assumed he was happy, but I wasn't entirely sure, so I asked the angels to send me a message if I was wrong.

I got ready to go to work and was just going out of the front door to put my long-haul suitcase outside when I saw feathers all over the place. Feathers can be a sign from angels. Just as I was wondering what they meant, I heard the front door lock behind me.

I froze, as now I had evidence of my cat not being well. I had no keys on me, but luckily I had my mobile in my pocket. I called my work and explained I was locked out and needed to wait for my partner to send me the keys by taxi from work.

At work they said to call them back once I managed to get into the house. What I did instead was ask the taxi driver to wait and take me to the vet's.

Once we got there my heart sank as I was told that my cat had a fractured femur and needed an operation. The purring I had heard had apparently been a sign that the cat was distressed. It was only then that I learned that there are different types of purring in cats.

Sometimes, particularly when we need to take immediate action, spirit messages are very obvious to us. In this case the door locking behind me made the decision for me.

But sometimes when you receive a message from Heaven you must wait for events to fall into place to guide you where you have to be. If you ask Heaven to show you how to get there, though, you will be given messages that will direct you.

Balancing Yin and Yang

At this point I need to bring your attention back to yin and yang energy and the importance of balancing them when making a connection to Heaven.

Heaven energy is very yin when you are trying to communicate, especially through practices such as meditation and prayer, which are conducted in silence, and the energy of panic is very yang, especially if you are dealing with earthly matters like your job or your home. If you can balance that by gathering the yin energy and communicating with Heaven, you can create a change within yourself which will enable you to be receptive to the messages.

There are two yin factors that you must observe: synchronicity and your intuition. They work together, but you must give your intuition a chance to develop. We have been told that we only use 10 per cent of our brain. After asking the spirit world many times to show me how to use my other 90 per cent, I have realized that that 90 per cent is actually the spiritual energy within us.

When we have balanced out the yin and yang energies, we will find the Earth energy around us and our own

Human behaviour will combine with Heaven energy to guide us on our way and create luck for us.

Healing from the Animal Kingdom

Through my mediumship I have come to understand that the animal kingdom has great power and when we come in contact with animals, mutual healing takes place. Animals do have souls and their spirits often manifest when I do platform work in Spiritualist churches. Animals can reflect our own energy – some dogs can smell cancer in their owners, or pregnancy – and the mission of our companion animals is to be there for those moments when we are unwell.

If you adopt an animal and give it a good life, you will start creating luck. Your pet will also help you to express love. When you choose a pet, please pick one that can relate to humans, though. Some animals do need to be in their natural habitat. Rare birds are meant to fly and we can stop the clandestine trafficking if there is no demand. Adopt an animal that really needs you so that your spiritual energy will be balanced and you can heal each other.

When you treat an animal badly, it is the same as asking to learn life the hard way. They are looked after by Mother Universe and she doesn't look kindly on anyone who ill-treats her pets. Everything in nature vibrates on a spiritual level, so respect it all. Otherwise it's like oversleeping on your own dreams – it will take you longer to achieve them. What goes around comes around, and at the end of the day we all came here to learn to be good, so please behave!

This leads us on neatly to the subject of karma.

CHAPTER 16

UNDERSTANDING KARMA

I believe that karma is very simple – whatever good you do brings good into your life and, equally, any negative, selfish or harmful actions will bring negative energy to you. It is all part of the process of living the life you are supposed to live, but more than this, I think it is about learning. Think of it like this: you signed a contract before you arrived on the planet about what you were going to achieve in this life and how you would achieve it. You are here to make a difference in the world and there are no failures in life, only lessons that are intended to make you strong and achieve your best.

We all have a story to live and we are all unique. We must learn to respect the flow of events and circumstances in our lives. Comparing our lives to those of others is of no use, because it doesn't change who we are today, right here and right now.

If you don't like yourself, don't just passively accept it – know that you can change. Even if life seems hopeless and you can't see any light ahead, don't give up – never give up. Once you make that decision to change, help will come to you in abundance, because your unconscious will be focused. Look at it as a long-term process and be patient, but watch out for coincidences and enjoy the changes that take place each day.

Remember, too, that there is no such thing as a perfect life. Everyone struggles, everyone faces challenges both big and small, and the negative things are what teach you about the nature of existence. Someone who has never had to earn anything won't know the value of money. Someone who has never had to earn love won't know the value of a loving relationship. Our hard times can be some of the most valuable.

So accept there is a gift in whatever comes your way, but remember that you can control your destiny. This will help you learn to trust change and so eliminate the fear of living.

Discover Your Own Power

Finding out where you are and how you are treating yourself in this life is fundamentally important. You can either do this by yourself or with the help of a skilled teacher, such as a therapist or other healer. This will help you to discover your power. In turn, it will help you to change the addictions, compulsive behaviour and other habits that bring negativity into your life. And it will allow abundance, happiness and luck to flood your life like light.

Sometimes we need to overcome challenges that we have created ourselves. Usually we have many excuses for avoiding this, but if you smoke, drink or eat without any concern for your health, isn't it time for you to stop and think what type of karma you are creating? We all know that all these type of challenges are denial related – we just can't cope with the stress of life – but now is the time to change for the bettter. We all deserve longevity and to be part of our family's and friends' lives. Make your life amazing and be your own motivation, don't wait for a reason to do it.

When a feng shui consultant turns up at someone's house or business, their mission is to help break the negative patterns that have arisen and to transform them into positive ones. That consultant must be spiritually aware enough to absorb any spiritual negativity from their client and remove it from their living space by reading the ambience and breaking the unhelpful patterns, using all the three energies, Earth, Human and Heaven. And they must be strong enough to hold that negative energy then release it somewhere else via Heaven energy. I know several highly skilled consultants who have become ill because they couldn't hold this energy, it drained them.

When I arrive in a space I immediately begin feeling and analyzing the energy, trying to see what's causing the negativity in the person's life, so I can reprogram it.

Often this will only involve small changes and won't cost much money. The most important thing I can do is to show the client that positivity breeds positivity – we can all change and influence our karma for the better.

This leads us to a very important point: many people mistakenly believe that karma is fixed – once we are born, we are stuck on a certain path, which we cannot change or step off, no more than we could step off a high ridge with a plunging drop to left and right. In fact, our karma isn't fixed – it is changeable energy. Although we are on a path through life, the direction of that path is down to us, depending on what we think and believe and how we behave.

Karma is all about transformation and adaptation. This will become apparent to us when we are challenged in life, as we all will be. When that happens, it's best to take responsibility, stop making excuses or blaming the world and act for the best. If we accept things the way they are, even if they aren't the way we planned, and make the best of them, a new world will unveil itself in front of our eyes.

Let me give you an example. Back in 1987, I became very ill with an infection and just by chance my mother suggested that I go and see a healer. I came across a wonderful woman called Mrs Gessy Persico and after a few sessions and blessings from her I recovered just like magic.

Gessy and Mr Persico had so much love to give to others it was really inspiring. Both were helping run a charity, Nosso Lar, which cared for over 100 children who were either orphans or had been abandoned by their families. It was based in a small town called Limeira, which translates as 'Lime Tree', in the state of Sao Paulo in Brazil and had been in existence for over 50 years but was really struggling because of a lack of money and was in danger of being closed down. I felt so grateful to Gessy that I decided to help her and her husband and their amazing charity.

Gessy had a very calm, almost angelic energy and after spending some time with her I discovered that miracles really did happen. I also realized that we had to pay forward the miracles that came our way – do the same for others so the miracles could ripple outwards into the world.

I needed a miracle at that point because the sponsors I had lined up to support this needy charity had decided to withdraw their help. When I went back to London I was devastated, and decided to pray for strength to carry on and find the right way to proceed. I couldn't understand it: my intention had purely been to do good, so why had this happened? I couldn't find an answer to it, so decided to accept things as they were … and suddenly got my answer.

A very special friend, Louise Veys, told me that her uncle had passed away and left her some money to donate to her chosen charity and she had chosen Nosso Lar.

I decided to use feng shui to help the charity. My first move was to landscape the garden, which had been concreted over. I then dealt with a mobile phone mast nearby which was adversely affecting the building because it had too much fire energy in it. In fact, they had even had a fire in the building!

With the help of another feng shui expert, I redesigned the whole place and the difference was amazing. The charity immediately came to the attention of major corporations, including the community relations department of British Airways and international bodies like Unicef, and received some major donations which saved it from closing. I am particularly grateful for the help of the famous two Marys in British Airways and of Derek Stalham, who controlled all the accounts. We used the money to train and educate the children's parents and soon all but 46 out of over 100 kids were able to return home to their families. We built a school for the children who stayed, so they could get lots of attention and do their homework properly with the help of volunteer teachers, and they ended up doing better than kids at state schools with perfect homes!

I was so happy to help those children, but they helped me too. Their stories were unique and inspiring. An amazing lesson of hope was provided by a baby who arrived at the home after his mother had fed him on the alcohol that she had found in the family home because she did not have money to buy milk and was too proud to seek help. The alcohol had caused a lot of damage to his health, but he survived, although he was left with special needs. No one wanted to adopt him because of this, but eventually when he was 15 the reason behind this came to surface: one of his older sisters was able to come to Nosso Lar and adopt him. I do believe in happy endings.

Charity work can be hard, but the sense of achievement it brings and the fantastic energy from Heaven makes life worth living.

When you aim to do good, the universe will listen to your wishes and prayers. All you have to say is 'Higher Power, I am working for you – help me!' Trust that you will have an answer and accept with your heart the help you will get.

Another great way to get in touch with your Heaven energy is to send out a prayer for someone who doesn't know it. Incredibly, their soul will recognize you the next time you see them – even if you don't actually know them.

As an exercise to get your Human and Heaven energy flowing, if you encounter someone who doesn't seem happy, look at them and silently say 'Peace be with you.' You can even try it if someone is being rude to you, or arrogant, for example in the supermarket.

You will be surprised by how quickly a change will occur. This is because at the instant their soul receives your wish for peace, all the turmoil will move away to Heaven.

This exercise will also give you a lot of confidence in the power within you.

Improving Karma

Getting our Heaven energy flowing for the good of all is one thing, but what else can we do to improve our karma?

I think one of the most important things is to learn about ourselves and heal the past, so we can move on from the challenges that we have faced as we have moved through life. This could be with the help of a professional counsellor, or through talking to a friend, or via spiritual healing – there are many ways. The point is that the intention to change will also activate luck.

During this process we may feel angry about what has happened to us. Getting to the point of anger means that we have lived in denial for long time and our soul needs to jump out of the cage that we have placed around ourselves. We do need to take responsibility, but often we just vent our anger on the nearest available loved one. It is always easier to blame others for our misfortune. But whatever the experience, it was there to place us on the path we are on today and we have to forgive and move on.

If people have hurt us intentionally, that is karma for them to deal with, and remaining angry about it can only hurt us. Don't worry if an injustice has been committed, because the truth will show itself sooner or later. Trust life and move on quickly. If you want to feel sorry for yourself, 24 hours is long enough. After that, focus on pleasure rather than anger. I have realized that people can lose everything through anger, including the love of those around them, so it is vital to deal with the issue. It could be a hormonal problem or due to an imbalance in the physical body, but it is up to us to move beyond it.

I used to be angry because of lost opportunities in life, but now I have changed because I realized that they were meant to be there so that I could learn about those feelings and how damaging they could be. The most interesting thing was that I discovered I had created them myself! Anger is a choice, but I changed and you can change also.

Gratitude can be a good way of helping ourselves to release anger, receive love and explore compassion. Think of what is working in your life – or even your day – and be grateful for it.

Also, if you look at what other people are feeling and accept that we all make mistakes, you will be on the way to leaving anger behind and feeling true compassion.

Think compassion, love and above all forgiveness and you will also understand and improve your karma. These qualities are focused on the heart area and we need to bring them out without fear. By doing that we will create spiritual resilience and enhance our immune system, too. If you find forgiveness difficult, pray every day that you can go beyond whatever is holding you back. You don't need to be religious to do this – just say a prayer and remember that all the experiences you have had, good and bad, have been there for a reason.

People who are at peace with themselves have good karma. Those are the ones who can see beyond appearances or disabilities and straight to the human soul without judgement or envy. When you see a beggar or a person with special needs, don't turn away because they could be a great soul in disguise. Help when you are given the opportunity. You will know when it is your turn.

If your own physical body isn't in great shape, it is important to realize that your soul is perfect and you can still start creating luck – your thoughts have the power.

Sharing, too, has power. Life without sharing has no meaning, and that is in all areas, not just personally. Sharing also generates luck because when you share it means that you divide something in equal parts. This shows you aren't acting out of fear of not having enough and are trusting in life to provide. This will trigger abundance.

The Rules from Heaven

Just to sum up, here is a list of the rules we live by when we come to Earth:

1. *You will receive a body.* You may like it or hate it, but it will be yours for the entire period this time around.

2. *You will learn lessons.* You are enrolled in a full-time informal school called life. Each day in this school you will have the opportunity to learn lessons. You may like the lessons or think them irrelevant.

3. *There are no mistakes, only lessons.* Growth is a process of trial and error. The 'failed' experiments are as much a part of the process as the experiments that ultimately 'work'.

4. *A lesson is repeated until it is learned.* A lesson will be presented to you in various forms until you have learned it. Then you can go on to the next lesson.

5. *Learning lessons does not end.* There is no part of life that does not contain its lessons. If you are alive, there are lessons to be learned.

6. *'There' is no better than 'here'.* When your 'there' has become 'here' you will simply obtain another 'there' that again looks better than 'here'.

7. *Others are merely mirrors of you.* You cannot love or hate something about another person unless it reflects something you love or hate about yourself.

8. *What you make of your life is up to you.* You have all the tools and resources you need; what you do with them is up to you. The choice is yours.

9. *The answers lie inside you.* All you need to do is look, listen and trust.

10. *You will forget all this*.

CHAPTER 17

CREATING SPACE FOR CHANGE

So, now you know something about Earth, Human and Heaven energies, you can bring them all together to make room for the changes you want to occur in your life. If you have too much of the old, there is no room for the new to come in.

Keep a full day free for this, as this journey will be very much like a rollercoaster.

Size Matters

Start by looking around your home. Is there enough room for one person? Is there enough room for two? Three? It can really affect us when we outgrow our homes.

A small space can also be a serious problem when the energy does not circulate well. I have had many cases where the physical space has had an influence on the relationship of the occupants. Sometimes it is sad because you can see couples splitting up because they are suffocating each other, even though they still love each other. Always aim to have enough space to move around and not have someone on top of you all the time. We all need those quiet moments.

If you and your partner are living with either set of parents while saving up for your own place, this is very positive as long as it is for six months maximum. Don't let it go on longer than that. Psychologically, it will affect you.

If you realize that you are in too small – or too large – a house for your current needs, consider whether it's time to move on.

Wherever you are, the next thing to address is what your space is like.

Clutter and Cleanliness

I recommend that you start in the direction that represents the area of your life that you wish to change, no matter where it is. Whether it is a bathroom, bedroom, living room or kitchen, just go in and see what it is telling you.

Is it cluttered? Is it clean? Cleanliness is paramount – when you find dust and rubbish it is a clear sign of stagnancy, and that part of your life too will come to a halt. So get things moving by starting to clean, with courage and a focused mind.

At the same time, if you feel you have never really been shown how to love, this is your chance to learn.

The following process usually works with an ancestral influence.

1. If you have lost a relative you loved very much, I recommend that you get a picture of them and light a candle for them. Then ask them to guide you. The spiritual world wants to be of service to you during your journey on Earth and this way you will make a connection to that energy.

2. Now wait and see what happens next. Somehow you will get the evidence that you are getting help, then your confidence will rise and your life will start to move forward.

This exercise also works if you think that life ends here. I guarantee that it will give you a connection to Heaven energy and that fear of the future will leave you.

When you use Heaven energy, trust that you will get things right, especially emotionally. Remember that Earth and Human energy are subject to Heaven energy.

Back in your home, go through every room. What do you love? What has meanings and memories for you? Anything else only accumulates dust, so off it goes to the rubbish. Really! It is easy to go into denial and create a reason to keep things. You will know you have done that when you look around and everything still looks the same. But do you want your life to remain the same?

Minimalism is actually the first way of showing that you have no fear of life. Believe it or not, the more you have around you, the more you are craving security and hiding from life.

Another reason for having a lot of stuff can be because we are given things and/or are left things through an inheritance. Make sure these items are only with you on a temporary basis, unless they are things that you really want to have in your life.

The energy of your home will carry you forward and dictate your destiny, so make sure it can always move freely. If there is a heavy piece of furniture in a particular direction of your house, say your love area, and you have to walk round it all the time, what do you think your love life will be like? Also, if that heavy piece of furniture is difficult to move, then it will be difficult to get your love life moving as well.

When I was in Japan doing land research at the Mount Kishimoto temple in the city of Osaka, I met a very interesting lady, a Buddhist, who blessed me for my work. I was learning the language of nature and buildings, and she appreciated my respect for nature and very kindly told the translator to tell me that the most important thing that I needed to know was 'the happiest home is the empty home'.

How simple and honest is that? In Japan homes do have very little furniture and it makes sense to detach from having things around us just for the sake of it rather than because we love them.

People hiding from life do it very well, because you can't even find their homes. They isolate themselves behind trees and bushes, but in turn these cover the view from the windows, and in terms of energy that means these people have no vision of the future. The view in the front of a home should always be clear.

The Benefits of Tidying Your Life

It isn't healthy to live in the middle of clutter and mess; if our home becomes stagnant, the same will apply to our soul and in turn our health. Earth, Human and Heaven energies are interconnected and it is up to us to keep everything clean and fresh and keep the energy flowing.

We all tend to clean and tidy when we know someone is coming round, but tidiness is actually paramount for our connection with our soul. Whatever we have around us is the reflection of that soul.

Tidiness is also about committing to our self-esteem and telling ourselves we deserve to live well in a nice environment that we can be proud of.

So, every week, have a day of super tidying and dusting and also choose to work on a part of your house or apartment that needs an extra clean. Maybe one week clean the windows, the next the shower doors. Please note, though, that it isn't healthy to become compulsive about cleaning. There's no need to become addicted to the process. Once a week is enough!

Tidying your home – or workplace – obviously helps with the physical environment, but is mostly a spiritual experience. It will help you to clear the residue from the experiences that didn't go the way you expected and empower your soul to choose the path that you believe you deserve. Here you are working with Earth and Heaven energies.

When you find your willpower kicking in, that means that you are back in business. Your Human energy is being restored and you are reconnecting to yourself and to those around you. Cleaning your house, tidying your office, sorting out your bedroom and giving unwanted things away will also lead to renewed generosity: you will feel so happy to help others. This is what it feels like to have abundance – and the feeling of abundance will bring more abundance. Generosity and abundance go together.

So, tidying your environment will not only clear the space around you but also re-establish your relationship with your health, money, love and above all with your soul. It will help you to understand how you treat every area of your life and to break patterns in your subconscious.

Your determination to bring about change will result in the universe responding to you by bringing the opportunities that are supposed to be yours. They may be linked to your past or present, but will definitely be linked to your future.

When you start getting results from cleaning and tidying, you will become enthusiastic and will want to do it everywhere – at work, at home, in other people's homes(!) – and it will get you thinking more about what you really need to have in your life. Does it make sense to have so many things that you don't need? Are you trying to prove something? To others or to yourself? Life is simple if you accept who you are as a person and realize that you need to grow and expand as a soul, not as a consumer to prove you belong to the tribe.

When you are taking care of your space and making more room for yourself or others, you will automatically change your focus from negative to positive and will create luck in the process.

FINDING PEACE

One thing we all really need in our lives is peace, so here's one final exercise:

1. Find a space to be alone. Play relaxing music in the background and go and lie on the floor or carpet.

2. Let your mind flow as you breathe slowly, programming your thoughts to take you where you want to go.

3. Relax into the peace this brings.

I hope this book has set you on the path to creating luck. Everything is possible and everything can be conquered if you only believe, so don't hold back. Life is short. Seize the moment.

Best of luck.

And always remember:

Twenty-four Things to Always Remember and One Thing Never to Forget

Your presence is a present to the world.
You are unique and one of a kind.
Your life can be what you want it to be.
Take days just one at a time.

Count your blessings, not your troubles.
You will make it through whatever comes along.
Within you are so many answers.
Understand, have courage, be strong.

Don't put limits on yourself.
So many dreams are waiting to be realized.
Decisions are too important to leave to chance.
Reach for your peak, your goal, your prize.

Nothing wastes more energy than worrying.
The longer you carry a problem, the heavier it gets.
Don't take things too seriously.
Live a life of serenity, not a life of regrets.

Remember that a little love goes a long way.
Remember that a lot ... goes on for ever.
Remember that friendship is a wise investment.
Life's treasures are people ... together.

Realize that it is never too late
To do ordinary things in an extraordinary way.

Have health and hope and happiness.
Take the time to wish upon a star.

And don't ever forget...
For even one day... how very special you are.

MING-GUA NUMBERS

Year of birth	Male	Female
1930	7	8
1931	6	9
1932	2	1
1933	4	2
1934	3	3
1935	2	4
1936	1	8
1937	9	6
1938	8	7
1939	7	8
1940	6	9
1941	2	1
1942	4	2
1943	3	3
1944	2	4
1945	1	8

Year of birth	Male	Female
1946	9	6
1947	8	7
1948	7	8
1949	6	9
1950	2	1
1951	4	2
1952	3	3
1953	2	4
1954	1	8
1955	9	6
1956	8	7
1957	7	8
1958	6	9
1959	2	1
1960	4	2
1961	3	3

Year of birth	Male	Female
1962	2	4
1963	1	8
1964	9	6
1965	8	7
1966	7	8
1967	6	9
1968	2	1
1969	4	2
1970	3	3
1971	2	4
1972	1	8
1973	9	6
1974	8	7
1975	7	8
1976	6	9
1977	2	1
1978	4	2
1979	3	3
1980	2	4
1981	1	8
1982	9	6
1983	8	7
1984	7	8
1985	6	9
1986	2	1
1987	4	2
1988	3	3
1989	2	4

Year of birth	Male	Female
1990	1	8
1991	9	6
1992	8	7
1993	7	8
1994	6	9
1995	2	1
1996	4	2
1997	3	3
1998	2	4
1999	1	8
2000	9	6
2001	8	7
2002	7	8
2003	6	9
2004	2	1
2005	4	2
2006	3	3
2007	2	4
2008	1	8
2009	9	6
2010	8	7
2011	7	8
2012	6	9
2013	2	1
2014	4	2
2015	3	3
2016	2	4
2017	1	8

Year of birth	Male	Female
2018	9	6
2019	8	7
2020	7	8
2021	6	9
2022	2	1
2023	4	2

Year of birth	Male	Female
2024	3	3
2025	2	4
2026	1	8
2027	9	6
2028	8	7
2029	7	8

East or West?

Northern Hemisphere: East Person

Ming-gua number	Sheng Chi	Tien Yi	Yen Nien	Fu Wei	Huo Hai	Wu Kwei	Liu Sha	Chueg Ming
	Good	Good	Good	Good	Bad	Bad	Bad	Bad
1 Water	South-east	East	South	North	West	North-east	North-west	South-west
3 Wood	South	North	South-east	East	South-west	North-west	North-east	West
4 Wood	North	South	East	South-east	North-west	South-west	West	North-east
9 Fire	East	South-east	North	South	North-east	West	South-west	North-west

197

Northern Hemisphere: West Person

Ming-gua number	Sheng Chi	Tien Yi	Yen Nien	Fu Wei	Huo Hai	Wu Kwei	Liu Sha	Chueg Ming
	Good	Good	Good	Good	Bad	Bad	Bad	Bad
2 Earth	North-east	West	North-west	South-west	East	South-east	South	North
6 Metal	West	North-east	South-west	North-west	South-east	East	North	South
7 Metal	North-west	South-west	North-east	West	North	South	South-east	East
8 Earth	South-west	North-west	West	North-east	South	North	East	South-east

Southern Hemisphere: East Person

Ming-gua number	Sheng Chi	Tien Yi	Yen Nien	Fu Wei	Huo Hai	Wu Kwei	Liu Sha	Chueg Ming
	Good	Good	Good	Good	Bad	Bad	Bad	Bad
1 Water	North-east	East	North	South	West	South-east	South-west	North-west
3 Wood	North	South	North-east	East	North-west	South-west	South-east	West
4 Wood	South	North	East	North-east	South-west	North-west	West	South-east
9 Fire	East	North-east	South	North	South-east	West	North-west	South-west

Southern Hemisphere: West Person

Ming-gua number	Sheng Chi	Tien Yi	Yen Nien	Fu Wei	Huo Hai	Wu Kwei	Liu Sha	Chueg Ming
	Good	Good	Good	Good	Bad	Bad	Bad	Bad
2 Earth	South-east	West	South-west	North-west	East	North-east	North	South
6 Metal	West	South-east	North-west	South-west	North-east	East	South	North
7 Metal	South-east	North-west	South-west	West	South	North	North-east	East
8 Earth	North-west	South-west	West	South-east	North	South	East	North-east

THE 12 ANIMALS OF THE CHINESE HOROSCOPE

Animal	Year of Birth					
Rat	1948	1960	1972	1984	1996	2008
Ox	1949	1961	1973	1985	1997	2009
Tiger	1950	1962	1974	1986	1998	2010
Rabbit	1951	1963	1975	1987	1999	2011
Dragon	1952	1964	1976	1988	2000	2012
Snake	1953	1965	1977	1989	2001	2013
Horse	1954	1966	1978	1990	2002	2014
Goat	1955	1967	1979	1991	2003	2015
Monkey	1956	1968	1980	1992	2004	2016
Rooster	1957	1969	1981	1993	2005	2017
Dog	1958	1970	1982	1994	2006	2018
Pig	1959	1971	1983	1995	2007	2019

Animals: Good Combinations

Animals that will have good personal or working relationships:

Animal 1	Animal 2	Animal 3
Dragon	Rat	Monkey
Goat	Rabbit	Pig
Snake	Rooster	Ox
Tiger	Horse	Dog

Animals: Poor Combinations

Animals that should avoid personal or working relationships with each other:

Animal 1	Animal 2
Rat	Horse
Ox	Goat
Tiger	Monkey
Rabbit	Rooster
Dragon	Dog
Snake	Pig
Horse	Rat
Goat	Ox
Monkey	Tiger
Rooster	Rabbit
Dog	Dragon
Pig	Snake

RESOURCES

Creating Luck Workshops and consultancy

www.marcioamaral.com

Feng Shui

The Chue Foundation

This book just gives you an idea of what is possible. I do advise the use of Chue consultants if you decide to have your property looked at properly. www.chuefoundation.org
www.masterkwchan.com

Roger Green

He now teaches feng shui and the best and most complete course in nutritional healing in New York, explaining that

nature communicates and the food we eat is pure power. His courses include building design and the ancient relationship between building and nature expressed through sacred geometry.
www.fengshuiseminars.com

Chinese Astrology

Jillian Stott

Chinese horoscopes from Jillian Stott.
www.authenticfengshui.org.uk

Geopathic Stress

Peter Stott

I often recommend that clients contact Peter Stott for a geopathic stress consultation. His 'geopsychic measurements', taken with the aid of specific machines designed for this type of work, can lead to the easing of any stress relating to a plot of land and the spirit of the home. Water running under the home, for example, can lead to an imbalance.

Some places are very yin and just measuring the energy flow will enliven the yang energy and get things moving again.
www.authenticfengshui.org.uk

Spiritualism

In the UK I recommend *Psychic News* newspaper as a start and also *Two Worlds* magazine. They both carry information on Spiritualist churches, including the times of services and information on healing and mediumship.

For healing (free or give in kind), refer to the College of Psychic Studies.
www.collegeofpsychicstudies.co.uk

Anger Management

Anger can eat you from the inside and anger release can work miracles. Anger management consultations and workshops can be very effective, so if you can't do it on your own, sign up!

Dan Roberts

If you are in the UK, I recommend the workshops with Daniel Roberts. www.danroberts.com.

Cranio-sacral Therapy and Chakra Balancing

Frederic Matland

If you do not feel centred, Frederic Matland specializes in bringing the soul back into the body. As well as many

techniques, he also offers counselling with a difference: pure loving energy.
www.stoneriver.org

Weight Loss, General Health and Well-being

This is a different type of gym and you are not just a number, they take your objectives very seriously, whether you have a health problem or just want to feel better in yourself. The students are encouraged to support each other and the tutors are trained on a loving level to see everyone as an individual. www.powervibe.co.uk

JOIN THE HAY HOUSE FAMILY

As the leading self-help, mind, body and spirit publisher in the UK, we'd like to welcome you to our family so that you can enjoy all the benefits our website has to offer.

EXTRACTS from a selection of your favourite author titles

COMPETITIONS, PRIZES & SPECIAL OFFERS Win extracts, money off, downloads and so much more

LISTEN to a range of radio interviews and our latest audio publications

CELEBRATE YOUR BIRTHDAY An inspiring gift will be sent your way

LATEST NEWS Keep up with the latest news from and about our authors

ATTEND OUR AUTHOR EVENTS Be the first to hear about our author events

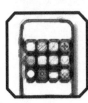

iPHONE APPS Download your favourite app for your iPhone

HAY HOUSE INFORMATION Ask us anything, all enquiries answered

join us online at **www.hayhouse.co.uk**

292B Kensal Road, London W10 5BE
T: 020 8962 1230 E: info@hayhouse.co.uk

We hope you enjoyed this Hay House book.
If you would like to receive a free catalogue featuring additional
Hay House books and products, or if you would like information
about the Hay Foundation, please contact:

Hay House UK Ltd
292B Kensal Road • London W10 5BE
Tel: (44) 20 8962 1230; Fax: (44) 20 8962 1239
www.hayhouse.co.uk

***

Published and distributed in the United States of America by:
Hay House, Inc. • PO Box 5100 • Carlsbad, CA 92018-5100
Tel: (1) 760 431 7695 or (1) 800 654 5126;
Fax: (1) 760 431 6948 or (1) 800 650 5115
www.hayhouse.com

***

Published and distributed in Australia by:
Hay House Australia Ltd • 18/36 Ralph Street • Alexandria, NSW 2015
Tel: (61) 2 9669 4299, Fax: (61) 2 9669 4144
www.hayhouse.com.au

***

Published and distributed in the Republic of South Africa by:
Hay House SA (Pty) Ltd • PO Box 990 • Witkoppen 2068
Tel/Fax: (27) 11 467 8904
www.hayhouse.co.za

***

Published and distributed in India by:
Hay House Publishers India • Muskaan Complex • Plot No.3
B-2• Vasant Kunj • New Delhi - 110 070
Tel: (91) 11 41761620; Fax: (91) 11 41761630
www.hayhouse.co.in

***

Distributed in Canada by:
Raincoast • 9050 Shaughnessy St • Vancouver, BC V6P 6E5
Tel: (1) 604 323 7100
Fax: (1) 604 323 2600

***

Sign up via the Hay House UK website to receive the Hay House
online newsletter and stay informed about what's going on with your
favourite authors. You'll receive bimonthly announcements
about discounts and offers, special events, product highlights,
free excerpts, giveaways, and more!
www.hayhouse.co.uk

ABOUT THE AUTHOR

 A natural medium, **Marcio Amaral** started developing in 1991 as a healer and bereavement counsellor at Stockwell Spiritualist Church, then joined the closed circle of the church to develop as a professional platform medium. For many years Marcio worked as a personal counsellor and healer on a one-to-one basis, helping people to overcome many difficulties and to accept themselves and their lives. He continued his training at the College of Psychic Studies. He was also part of the closed circle at the prestigious London Spiritual Mission, and now trains with Anthony Kesner in an advanced class alongside many very gifted mediums.

Marcio became interested in feng shui studies after meeting a consultant whilst working to put himself through university. At that point he realised that he had found his true cause in life and left all studies to follow these teachings and take an accreditation with Roger Green. Between 1999 and 2002, he ran a series of corporate feng shui workshops in the UK.

Now with two accreditations, Marcio belongs to the Chue Foundation representing Brazil, and also consults in Mexico, USA and London. He helps clients both with feng shui and the three energies, and with his mediumship expertise, which includes their personal emotions. This dual approach makes him unique among feng shui consultants. He is now furthering his studies with Great Grand Master Chan.

Marcio frequently demonstrates his mediumship on a charitable basis in many churches around the UK, helping to raise awareness of life after death and the spiritual movement. He is Ambassador for the charity Nosso Lar in Limeira, Brazil, and raises funds for many animal and children's charities in the UK. In Marcio's view, social contributions are paramount to a successful karmic life. The variety of spiritual studies and the relationship between energy and spirituality has always fascinated Marcio. His Creating Luck workshops help people to shift their thought patterns, to see life as energy and to become more independent emotionally.

www.marcioamaral.com